BRIGHT iDEAS

Science Projects

GW00862591

Written by Frances Mackay

Published by Scholastic Publications Ltd,
Villiers House,
Clarendon Avenue,
Leamington Spa,
Warwickshire CV32 5PR

© 1995 Scholastic Publications
Text © 1995 Frances Mackay

Author Frances Mackay
Editor Noel Pritchard
Assistant Editor Kate Banham
Designers Clare Brewer and Tracey Ramsey
Illustrations by Gay Galsworthy
Cover design by Lynda Murray
Cover photograph by Martyn Chillmaid
Designed using Aldus Pagemaker
Processed by Pages Bureau, Leamington Spa
Artwork by Castle Graphics, Kenilworth
Printed in Great Britain by Clays Ltd, St Ives plc

British Library Cataloguing-in-Publication Data
A catalogue record for this book is available from the British Library.

ISBN 0-590-53323-1

The right of Frances Mackay to be identified as the Author of this work has been asserted by her in accordance with the Copyright, Designs and Patent Act 1988.

Contents

Introduction

The Science National Curriculum involves the use of AT1, Experimental and Investigative Science, to explore and investigate the other main themes of Science – Life and living processes, Materials and their properties and Physical processes. These main themes can be conveniently grouped into topics which teachers can use as a basis for a whole range of cross-curricular activities within the primary classroom.

A science topic is often used by teachers as a basis for a half-term or whole term's programme of work as it lends itself so well to a cross-curricular approach. The topics in this book have been chosen with this purpose in mind, although the activities could, of course, be taught as part of a series of separate science lessons if the teacher so desires.

USING THIS BOOK IN SCHOOL

This book could be used to support the teaching and learning of science in many ways:
• Each chapter could form the basis for planning a term's topic. Links to other subject areas are provided at the end of each chapter to help with such planning.
• It could be used as a resource bank to supplement topics already in progress in the classroom.
• It could be used as the basis for a short, intense programme of scientific investigations.
• It could be used to help develop separate lesson plans for science work.
• It could be used as a support programme for children to use when other science work has been completed or as an extension of particular work in progress.

• It could be used as lesson 'one-offs' when other set work has been completed.

THE CONTENT OF THE BOOK

The book is divided into eight chapters, each covering a particular topic or theme. The theme could be developed equally well in either Key Stage 1 or Key Stage 2 classrooms.

Each chapter follows the same format:
• A brief introduction explains how the topic can be used for science studies and provides possible ideas for developing the topic.
• An age range is provided to indicate the main target group for each activity, but in many cases the possible age range is wider and teachers could adapt activities as appropriate.

• A group size is provided to indicate the suggested number of pupils participating in an activity but again, this could easily be adapted.

• A science content section outlines the concepts covered by each activity. Some of the information may be beyond the level of understanding of most children, but will give the teacher confidence to ask and answer questions and guide the children in their investigations.

• The 'What you need' section specifies the resources required for each activity.

• The 'What to do' section outlines what the teacher needs to do to set up the activity and what the children may be required to do in order to complete the task.

• The follow-up section provides some suggestions for activities which could follow on from the main task.

Some activities also have photocopiable pages to accompany them. The activities will explain how these are to be used, and the photocopiable section can be found at the end of the book.

At the end of each chapter are some ideas on display and a page of suggested cross-curricular activities linked to the theme of the chapter. The display ideas are intended to provide suggestions for how the activities could be displayed in the classroom, together with other work completed by the children. The page of suggested links with other subjects can be used as a planning tool for developing a wider study of the topic.

ASSESSMENT IDEAS

The new National Curriculum guidelines for Science require the teacher to assess a child's work according to a set of level descriptions. These level descriptions describe 'the types and range of performance which pupils working at a particular level should characteristically demonstrate.' Teachers are

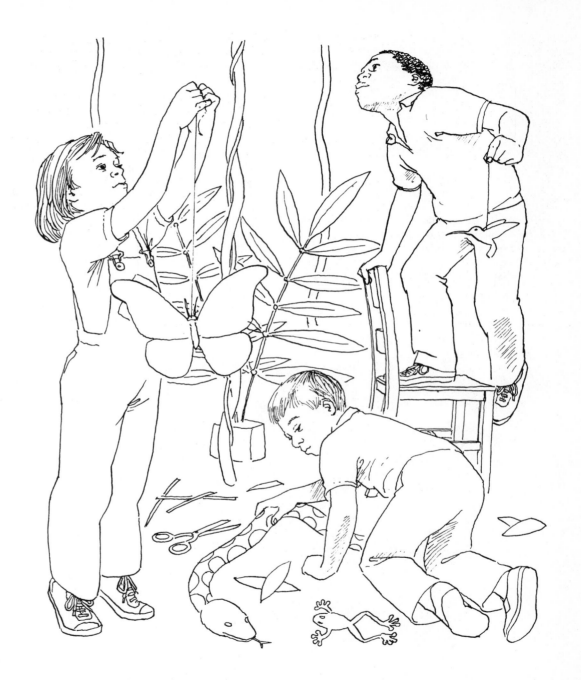

asked to judge which level best fits a child's performance.

Such assessment is required at the end of a key stage but teachers will also want to assess children's work as part of an ongoing evaluation of science in their classrooms in order to:
• provide feedback to the children in the form of informal praise or encouragement and written comments;
• discover where the child is already at in order to further the child's progress;
• appraise and report individual progress to parents.

Many of the activities described in this book could be used as part of this ongoing assessment and there are many procedures which teachers can adopt in order to achieve this. These include:
• using an independent observer to make written comments;
• using tape or video recordings;
• using checklists;
• using oral evidence from conferences with the child;

• photographing children's work;
• developing pupil profiles/portfolios;
• using structured tasks such as SATs or formal tests;
• using the children's own self-assessment;
• using written/diagrammatic evidence.

All of the above have a place in the assessment of children's work in science but perhaps most useful of all is the last one, the use of written or diagrammatic evidence.

Notes, diagrams and drawings provide a permanent record of the investigation and can be used for immediate assessment and discussion or for future discussions with the child. Diagrams and drawings provide an appropriate method of communication when writing skills are less developed and also serve as an invaluable insight into the child's thinking and observational skills. Notes and diagrams also allow the teacher to sample group work without directly observing each child.

Asking the children to write down or draw what they know before commencing a task can be very worthwhile because it provides

the teacher with an insight into the knowledge and skills already possessed by each child. Comparisons can then be made between this writing and writing conducted at the end of the activity or series of activities. It is important to remember, however, that children do not always accurately write or draw what they actually think or observe and hence the teacher must always discuss the work with the child and use it as just one way of obtaining information about that child.

Concept mapping is one way of obtaining a summative form of assessment. These maps are used to demonstrate the child's understanding of the relationships between things without having to write lengthy, detailed descriptions. Two examples are given below.

Together with the teacher's own observations of a child, such notes, diagrams and drawings will help the teacher to decide on a pupil's level of attainment in science.

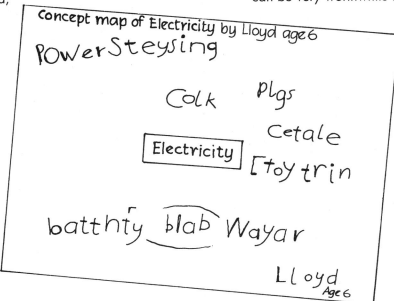

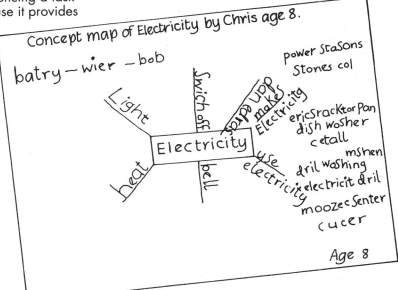

Ourselves

This topic holds a fascination for all age groups. Most children are interested in how their bodies work and find learning about what is inside their body intriguing. It also has a very important role to play in developing an awareness of how to stay fit and healthy. Encouraging young children to be aware of personal hygiene, healthy foods and the importance of exercise may pave the way for a much healthier adult lifestyle and, as such, may have many lasting future benefits.

Older children can also be introduced to some of the body systems which help us to function properly such as digestion, blood circulation, skeletal and muscular systems and reproduction. If children at primary level are informed about the harmful effects of tobacco, alcohol and other drugs, it may help prevent them from experimenting with these drugs in later life.

Growing up

Age range
Five to seven.

Group size
Individuals or pairs.

What you need
Magazine pictures showing the stages of human development (babies, young children, teenagers, adults), adhesive, scissors, paper or card.

Science content
Humans grow from babies into children and then into adults. Adults can produce babies. All humans grow old.

What to do
Ask the children to sort the pictures into chronological order from babyhood to old age. They can then stick the pictures on to paper or card so that it represents a 'time-line' of human development. Encourage the children to share their results with others. Ask them to give reasons for their choices, for example, how they can tell a teenager from someone in their twenties. Help them to decide on the ages by looking closely at certain clues such as clothing styles, hair colouring, wrinkles and so on. Discuss similarities and differences between the people in the pictures and the children themselves.

Follow-up
The children could be asked to bring in photographs of themselves from babyhood to the present day. Encourage them to talk about the way they have changed – likes and dislikes, hair colouring, height, weight and so on. They

could make up their own personal file which could include information about themselves at present – weight, height, shoe size and so on – and then record those measurements again at intervals throughout the year to see how much they have changed. They could also be asked to predict how they see themselves in the future – what they think they will look like, what things they might like to do.

Body parts

Age range
Five to seven.

Group size
Individuals.

What you need
Photocopiable page 117, scissors, adhesive, paper, thin card.

Science content
An introduction to the following external body parts – head, neck, chest, waist, hip, leg, knee, foot, arm, elbow, hand.

What to do
Photocopy page 117 directly on to thin card or stick a copy of the page to thin card. Depending on the age and ability of the children, either cut out the jigsaw pieces for them or ask them to cut out the pieces themselves. Explain that the jigsaw makes up a picture of a person and ask them to piece it together correctly. Once completed, the puzzle could be stuck to paper as a permanent picture, or the pieces stored in a plastic bag to be used again.

   Discuss the completed puzzle with the children. Can they name all the body parts? Can they point to these parts on their own body? Play games such as 'Simon Says' to reinforce the names of the body parts.

Follow-up
Discuss with the children what we use these body parts for. Talk about how our body moves – joints such as jaw, knees, elbow; muscles such as face and legs and so on. Ask the children to make a list or draw pictures of things we can do with each of the body parts on the photocopiable page. Include some of these movements in PE or dance activities.

Me and my friend

Age range
Six to eight.

Group size
Pairs.

What you need
Photocopiable page 118, a pencil, mirror, coloured pencils, bathroom scales, height measuring stick.

Science content
This activity encourages children to recognise the similarities and differences between themselves and other pupils. It will help them to understand that everyone is unique.

What to do

Ask the children to sit with a friend and use a mirror to look at their own facial features, noting such things as eye, skin and hair colour and any special features such as freckles. Ask them to draw a picture of themselves and their friend in the space provided on the worksheet and to fill in the sections about eye, hair and skin colour.

Help each pair to measure their height and weight and to record this on the sheet. Each child can then write about or draw the things they and their friend most like to do.

Follow-up

Ask the children to bring in photographs of themselves and their family. Put the pictures on display and ask the children to find similarities and differences between themselves and their family members. (If this is a sensitive issue, the children could cut out pictures of people in magazines and note the differences between themselves and the people in the pictures.) This could lead on to a study of people in other countries and similarities and differences could be drawn between these people and themselves. A list of features all humans have in common could be compiled and then comparisons made between humans and other animals.

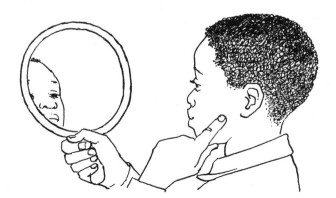

My senses

Age range

Six to eight.

Group size

Groups of five or six.

What you need

Activity 1: six plastic cups, each containing a sample of orange, lemon, onion, vinegar, coffee, tea; a blindfold.
Activity 2: different flavoured crisps, a blindfold.
Activity 3: a 'feely' bag or box.
Activity 4: six sealed tins containing coins, rice, modelling clay, a ping-pong ball, pebbles and sand.
Activity 5: three cards with large 'C's (about 2cm tall) on them, a metre ruler.

Science content

Humans use their senses to learn things about the world around them.

The top part of the nose has nerve endings which are sensitive to chemicals dissolved in the moist air of the nasal passages. The nerves send messages to the brain which interprets what the smells are.

Taste is closely related to smell. Parts of the tongue are covered in taste buds which are stimulated by various chemical substances dissolved in saliva. Sweet and salty tastes are detected most at the tip of the tongue, sour at the sides and bitter at the back.

When things vibrate they make sounds causing sound waves to pass into the ear canal. The eardrum vibrates, sending impulses along the nerves to the brain.

The lens in the eye helps to focus images on the retina. Sometimes this image is imperfect and glasses are needed.

guess what it is. (*Safety:* Ensure that there are no sharp or pointed objects put into the bag.) Record the results.

Activity 4: Ask the children to guess what the objects are inside the tins by rattling them. They should record all their guesses by drawing or writing. You can reveal the answers when all the groups have finished the activity.

Activity 5: Ask one partner to hold up a card while the other partner stands two metres away and closes one eye. She should look at the card and use her hand to point in the direction the C is pointing (left, right, up or down). She can then try her other eye, while her partner points the C in a different direction. Tell the child to move back one metre each time she looks at the C, until she no longer gets the correct answer. Ask the children to record this distance.

Follow-up

Find out about things that can go wrong with our senses and how people overcome the difficulties which arise – such as the use of Braille for blind people and sign language for the deaf. Discuss how to look after our eyes, mouth, nose, ears and hands, and relate this to hygiene, health and safety.

What to do

Arrange the class into five equal groups. The whole class can then work through the five activities in rotation or, alternatively, prepare one activity for each day of the week and each group can take turns to perform that activity throughout the day.

Activity 1: Ask the children to take turns to wear the blindfold and see if they can guess the foods in the cups by smell alone. Each group could record the results in some way, perhaps by drawing all the foods they guessed correctly.

Activity 2: Ask the children to take turns to wear the blindfold and guess the flavour of the crisp put into their mouth by a partner. They could record their results in the same way as in Activity 1. (*Safety:* During all tasting activities great care should be taken to ensure hygiene and avoid activating allergies.)

Activity 3: Ask each child in the group to find a small object in the classroom and hide it in their pocket. They can then take turns to place the object in the bag while the others

Healthy food

Age range
Seven to nine.

Group size
Individuals or pairs.

What you need
Paper plates, paper, crayons, scissors, adhesive, pictures or real examples of: bread, cereal, vegetables, fruit, water (Group A); milk, fish, meat/poultry, eggs, nuts, cheese (Group B); sugar, oil, margarine/butter (Group C).

Science content
To stay healthy we need certain types of food each day – two or three servings of Group A, one serving of Group B and very small amounts of Group C.

What to do
Display pictures or, if possible, the real foods in the three groups. Discuss with the children the following things – their favourite foods, what they usually have for breakfast and lunch, how many drinks they have a day and what these are, what foods they eat when they want a snack. (Some of this information could be recorded in graph form later or put on to a suitable database computer program.) Go on to talk about the foods in each of the groups and how much of each type of food is recommended to stay healthy. Ask the children to plan a healthy meal by drawing the foods, colouring them and sticking them on to the paper plates. Display these on a table with a table-cloth and cutlery.

Follow-up
Ask the children to keep a food diary of all the foods eaten in one day/week (written or pictorial). They can use the diary to determine whether or not they have a healthy diet. Ask the children to survey school meals and foods available at the tuck shop (if these are on the school premises) and sort the foods into healthy and not so healthy groups. Finally, the children can design posters to encourage other children to eat healthily.

Pulse rate

Age range
Eight to eleven.

Group size
Pairs.

What you need
A stopwatch or watch with a second hand, a pencil, paper, bench or chair.

Science content
The heart acts as a pump, pushing blood around the body. The blood contains food and oxygen for the muscles and organs. Each time the heart beats it is called a heartbeat. The beats can best be felt at the wrist or neck. The beats are called a pulse. During exercise the pulse rate increases in order for the muscles to obtain enough food and oxygen necessary for the work they need to do.

What to do
Talk about the function of the heart with the children and how it pumps blood around the body. Ask them to tell you why they think we need the blood to move around our bodies. Next, talk about the pulse and how it can be felt. Ask the children to use their fingers, not their thumb, to feel the pulse on their wrist or neck.

Explain that they are going to investigate how our pulse rate changes. Ask each child to count the number of beats they can feel in half a minute while resting. Use a stopwatch to time this. They can then double this score to find out how many times their heart beats in one minute. Then ask them to count their pulse as soon as they have completed each of the following activities:

- 20 arm swings;
- 40 step-ups;
- running for two minutes.

(For step-ups, ask one child to hold a chair or bench steady while their partner steps up and down.)

Ask the children to record their results in some way – perhaps in the form of a graph or table. How much do their results vary? Do different children have different numbers of beats? Does the pulse rate increase with each exercise? Can the children explain why the heart needs to beat faster when we are exercising? How long does it take for the heart to return to the resting pulse rate? Is this the same for everyone?

Follow-up
Ask some adults to complete the same activity. What comparisons can be made with the children's results? Do adults who exercise regularly have different results from those who do not? Why could this be?

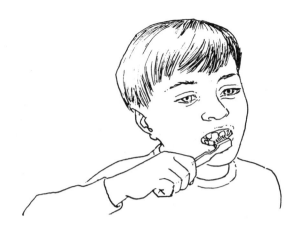

Teeth and dental care

Age range
Seven to nine.

Group size
Four to six.

What you need
Hand mirrors, dental disclosing tablets, a toothbrush, model teeth (optional), clean modelling clay, dental floss.

Science content
The average adult has 32 teeth and young children have 20 teeth. There are four types of teeth and each type does a different job – incisors bite and cut food; canines hold and tear food and premolars and molars grind and crush food. The outer layer of the tooth is called enamel and this forms a hard, biting surface. Plaque eats away at teeth and gums so regular brushing is necessary. Teeth should be cleaned across the gums, down from the gums and between the teeth. Dental floss aids in cleaning between the teeth.

What to do
Ask the children to use a hand mirror to look at their own teeth. Can they count how many they have? Do they have any gaps or fillings? Ask them to look at the shapes of the teeth. Are the front ones different from the back ones? Can the children suggest why? Discuss the names of the types of teeth and their uses with the children. Ask them to write down how many incisors, canines, premolars and molars they have. Compare the group's answers. Explain that the number of teeth varies greatly between children and adults and that some people will have more teeth than others.

The children can use clean modelling clay to make a cast of their teeth to obtain a better understanding of their shape, size and number. Use these casts or a model of teeth and a toothbrush to discuss with the children how to clean their teeth correctly. Ask them to demonstrate how they should use the brush. Do they all agree? Mention brushing in between the teeth and show them some dental floss, demonstrating how to use it.

How often do the children think they should visit a dentist and why is it important? Talk about the kinds of foods which are good for our teeth and those which are bad.

Finally, the children can chew a disclosing tablet to see where plaque gathers. This will help them understand where they need to brush their teeth.

Follow-up
• Make posters telling people how to care for their teeth.
• Compare the teeth of humans with other animals. Are the teeth of herbivores different from those of carnivores? Why?

Our bones

Age range
Nine to eleven.

Group size
Pairs.

What you need
Photocopiable page 119, reference books on the human skeleton, a measuring tape, height measuring stick.

Science content
Some animals, including humans, have skeletons and muscles to support their bodies and help them move. The bones also provide protection for internal organs. The human skeleton has 206 bones.

What to do
Provide the children with photocopiable page 119 and discuss the bones in the diagram. Ask the children to feel their ribs and their arm and finger bones. Can they estimate

how many bones there are in their fingers (14). Let them compare the sizes of their bones by working with a partner and measuring their finger, leg, arm lengths and so on. Ask them to complete the questions on photocopiable page 119. Compare results with the rest of the class. The distances between 1 and 2 and 4, 5 and 6 should be approximately the same (especially in adults) because our body parts are in proportion to each other. Ask the children to give possible reasons for the results.

Finally, ask the children to use reference books to find out:
• how many bones there are in our body (*206*);
• what the body part which joins two bones together is called (*joint*);
• how the muscles are joined to the bones (*by tendons*);
• why our bodies need a skeleton (*to protect and support the soft internal organs and to provide places of attachment for muscles to help movement*);
• what the medical names for the bones in the diagram are (*skull – cranium, collar bone – clavicle, shoulder blade – scapula, breast bone – sternum, rib – rib, upper arm – humerus, back bone – lumbar vertebra, lower arm – radius and ulna, hip bone – pelvis, wrist – carpals, hand bones – metacarpals and phalanges, thigh bone – femur, knee cap – patella, lower leg – tibia and fibula, ankle – tarsals, foot bones – metatarsals and phalanges*).

Follow-up
• Let the children study skeletons of other animals by looking at models or diagrams in books. Ask them to compare them to human skeletons. What similarities and differences are there?
• If possible, ask the children to do observational drawings of real bones (many secondary schools have these) and encourage them to consider such things as strength, size, shape, how bones join together and so on.

Our heart

Age range
Nine to eleven.

Group size
Two to four.

What you need
A diagram or model of the human heart (showing the different chambers), a sheep's heart (you should be able to get one of these from a butcher), paper, a pencil, knife, chopping board.

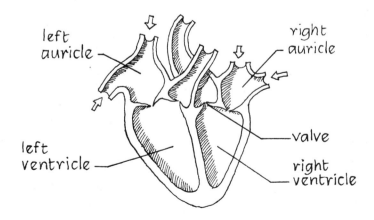

left auricle

right auricle

left ventricle

valve

right ventricle

Science content
The heart is part of the circulatory system which also includes the arteries, veins and blood. The heart pumps blood around the body. The blood contains food and oxygen for the muscles and organs. Arteries carry the blood away from the heart, and veins carry the blood back to the heart.

What to do
Show the children the picture or model of the human heart. Do they know where their heart is? Can they tell you what it does? Explain that the heart acts like a big pump, pushing blood around the body. Can the children suggest why blood needs to travel around the body?

Now, ask the children to look at the veins on their arms. Explain to them that veins carry blood to the heart and arteries carry it away. Look at the diagram of the heart, pointing out the different chambers. Explain that there are special valves in the heart which stop the blood from flowing backwards.

Next, look at the sheep's heart. Is its shape what the children expected it to be? Is its size what they expected? Carefully cut the heart open to look at the chambers inside. Pay particular attention to the thickness of the walls. Can the children suggest why they are so thick? Can the children see the valves? Allow them time to do some observational drawings of the sheep's heart.

Finally, ask them to draw and/or write about how the human heart works and how arteries and veins carry blood around the body.

Follow-up
Challenge the children to make a working model of the circulatory system, including the heart, arteries and veins, using transparent plastic bottles and tubing with coloured water.

Healthy lifestyle

Age range
Nine to eleven.

Group size
Individuals or whole class.

What you need
Photocopiable page 120, books on health and fitness.

Science content
This activity will provide a stimulus for whole class or group discussion about how to stay healthy. It will encourage children to think about their own lifestyles and may help them to understand how they can improve their chances of staying healthy.

What to do
Explain to the class that they are going to carry out a survey to find out how healthy their lifestyle is. Provide each child with a copy of photocopiable page 120 and ask them to complete the survey.

Once completed, allow them time to discuss their answers with a friend or in a small group to see if they agree on some of their answers, such as the importance of washing hands, the use of other people's medicines and so on.

Next, bring the whole class together to discuss the results. A tally chart could be made to record some of the answers, for example: How many times a week do you exercise? Does anyone in your family smoke? Do you eat fruit and vegetables every day? This can be used to ascertain whole class responses.

It is important to discuss each question either as a whole class or in groups so that you can explain the importance of a healthy diet and regular exercise, and the dangers of drug abuse. Some questions need sensitivity, such as asking whether someone in the family smokes, so you will need to be aware of this.

The children can use the information gathered from the discussion, together with any reference books you can provide, to make up a timetable for a week showing the ideal foods, amount of rest and exercise and any other ideas that a child could follow in order to stay healthy. Perhaps they could then try out their weekly timetable themselves to see what happens and discuss the outcomes with others.

Follow-up
• Ask the children to make posters of ways to stay healthy and fit.
• Conduct a survey of the school tuck shop or school meals – are they healthy? Can they be improved?
• What games do children play at break times? Could other activities be introduced to encourage the children to exercise more?

Digestion

Age range
Ten to eleven.

Group size
Small groups or whole class.

What you need
Reference books showing the digestive system in humans or a model of the digestive system.

Science content
Digestion breaks down the many compounds in food into different elements which the body uses to nourish tissues and to provide us with energy. Digestion reduces the food to a soluble state which can easily pass through cell membranes.

The process begins in the mouth where food is chewed by the teeth and mixed with saliva. It then travels down the oesophagus, helped by muscular movements called peristalsis. In the stomach, hydrochloric acid breaks down the food into a creamy fluid. The food can stay here for one or two hours. It then passes into the small intestine where fluids from the pancreas and liver help to break it down further. It is now ready to be absorbed. The small intestine is covered with small villi which are richly supplied with blood vessels. The digested food passes into these blood vessels and it is carried to the body cells which use the food to provide energy. Water is absorbed in the large intestine and solid wastes leave the body through the rectum.

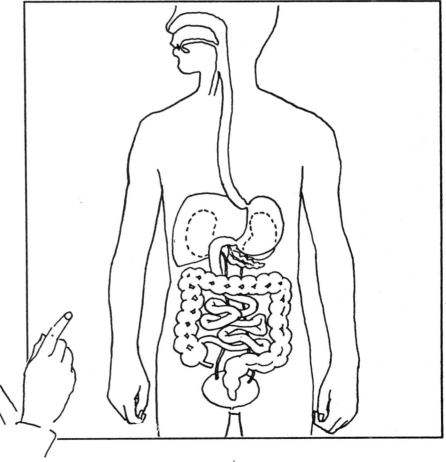

What to do

The way that energy is actually released from the food is a very difficult thing to explain and all children need to know at this level is how the digestive system works and what the food is used for.

Ask the children to give reasons for why they think we have to eat. Can they say how this food provides us with energy? Ask them to tell you what they think happens to the food once we have chewed and swallowed it. Can they name any of the body parts which help digestion?

Explain the process of digestion from the mouth through each body part, using books or a model to show what these parts look like and where they are in relation to each other. Ask the children to point to where their oesophagus, stomach, liver and intestines are on their own body. The children could then draw their own diagrams of the digestive system and write down in their own words what happens to the food they eat.

Follow-up

The children could find out about the digestive system of other mammals, such as the cow, and how this differs from their own system. They could also study the effects of acids (such as vinegar) on foodstuffs to help them understand how food is broken down.

DISPLAY IDEAS

• Ask children to bring in photographs of themselves at various ages. Photocopy them or use the actual photographs to make a display. Can the children identify each other from the photographs? What changes can they spot between the photographs of each individual as they have grown older?

• Trace around the body outline of several children on to large pieces of paper. Use the outlines for various activities such as filling them with body words, drawing in body organs or showing the difference in height between the tallest and shortest child (this may need to be handled sensitively). You could also cut out drawings of body parts to fit the outline and ask the children to put them in the right place.

• Make individual books about each child – containing photographs, information about themselves, body measurements, self-portraits, and so on. Display these books with posters and pictures showing people at different stages of development.

• Make clay models of children in the class. Display these models alongside paintings and drawings of people in the class.

• Make a mural of letters of the alphabet and on each large letter shape write down the names of body parts, organs, things we can do with our bodies and so on that begin with the designated letter.

• Make mobiles of skeletons and hang them in a breezy spot.

Links with other curriculum areas

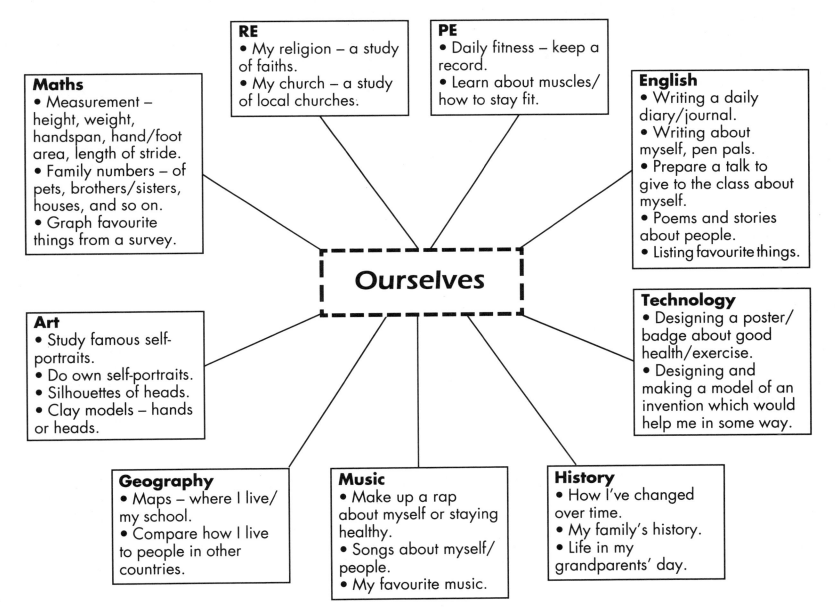

RE
• My religion – a study of faiths.
• My church – a study of local churches.

PE
• Daily fitness – keep a record.
• Learn about muscles/ how to stay fit.

Maths
• Measurement – height, weight, handspan, hand/foot area, length of stride.
• Family numbers – of pets, brothers/sisters, houses, and so on.
• Graph favourite things from a survey.

English
• Writing a daily diary/journal.
• Writing about myself, pen pals.
• Prepare a talk to give to the class about myself.
• Poems and stories about people.
• Listing favourite things.

Ourselves

Technology
• Designing a poster/ badge about good health/exercise.
• Designing and making a model of an invention which would help me in some way.

Art
• Study famous self-portraits.
• Do own self-portraits.
• Silhouettes of heads.
• Clay models – hands or heads.

Geography
• Maps – where I live/ my school.
• Compare how I live to people in other countries.

Music
• Make up a rap about myself or staying healthy.
• Songs about myself/ people.
• My favourite music.

History
• How I've changed over time.
• My family's history.
• Life in my grandparents' day.

Living things

This topic is a very popular theme for science activities because it centres very much on firsthand experience and the use of the local environment. It is important that children are made aware of the delicate balance of nature and how plants, animals and humans all play a vital role in maintaining this balance.

Children should be taught how to handle plants and animals in a sensitive way and how to study an aspect of the environment without causing undue harm to the living things which reside there. The links between living things can be illustrated through the study of food chains, predator/prey relationships and the effects that humans can have on their environment.

It is important for children to study several different habitats to develop an awareness of the huge variety of living things that exist and the differences and similarities between them.

Flowering plant parts

Age range
Five to seven.

Group size
Two to four.

What you need
Paper, a pencil, flowers, flowering house plants, hand lenses, reference books.

Science content
Most green plants have leaves to help in photosynthesis, a stem to provide support, roots to obtain water and nutrients and flowers to reproduce.

What to do
Provide the children with a variety of plants. Ask them to look very closely at them using a hand lens. Encourage the children to observe the following things – colours, shapes, textures, smells, number of petals, number and shape of leaves and so on.

Ask them to name as many parts as they can, then use reference books to help them find out the names of other parts. Encourage them to observe similarities and differences between the plants.

If possible, provide three examples of the same plant. Ask the children to compare the number of leaves, colours, shapes, textures and so on of these three plants. This will help them realise that the plants may look very similar but that each is unique. Reference could be made here to humans – how we are very alike yet very different. The children could then be encouraged to group the plants in some way of their own choosing and to give reasons for these groupings. This will help develop skills necessary in the use of identification keys.

Follow-up

Visit a garden so the children can see a wider variety of plants. Encourage them to consider the trees and grasses also and to find similarities and differences between these and the plants they have studied in the classroom. If possible, allow the children an opportunity to grow and care for their own plants – spider plants are ideal for this as they are very quick and easy to grow.

Wildlife walk

Age range
Five to seven.

Group size
Whole class.

What you need
Hand lenses, plastic jars with lids, magnispectors, pooters, plastic spoons, plastic bags, identification books of plants and animals, clipboards, paper, crayons, small pieces of card painted with different shades of blue, green, yellow and brown (enough for one piece per child).

Science content
The aim of the walk is to make the children aware that both plants and animals are living things and that a huge variety of both exist.

What to do
Choose a suitable site that is close to the school – the school's wildlife area if you have one, a nearby wood or waste ground or a garden. Explain to the children that the purpose of the walk is to look at all the plants and animals they see and to draw some of them.

It is vital to stress to the children the importance of caring for the things they may capture or view. Before the walk, discuss the following things with the children: the need to walk quietly and carefully, to return creatures quickly to where they were found after they have been looked at and to replace stones and leaves as they were found. Also, before setting out, ensure that the children know how to use the lenses and containers. Allow them time to play with them and try lifting things using the spoons or screwing up lids and so on. This will help to ensure the children's interest on the walk is not centred on the equipment itself but what they find.

If other adults are accompanying you on the walk, make sure they know the kinds of questions to ask the children that will help develop their understanding of living things, such as: Are the plants all green? Where are the insects found? Are the leaves the same shape? How many colours can you find? How many living things can you find on one tree? Do different plants grow in shady and sunny places? How many legs do the insects have? Can you see any animal tracks? Can you see any animal homes? Can you find an animal eating something?

Provide each child with a coloured piece of card. Ask them to match up the colour with some living thing along the walk. This will help them to focus on the walk and will also show the wide variety of colours in nature. Take photographs so that the finds can be 'captured' for later study.

Stop occasionally to let the children use the lenses and equipment to capture small animals and take a closer look. Let them draw the creatures and use books to help identify them. Don't forget also to look at plants.

In all of the above activities stress the importance of making the tests fair.

Follow-up
Hold another walk in a very different setting to compare the living things found there. Display photographs and drawings of the things found by the children and make up a list of the differences and similarities between the two places.

Growing plants

Age range
Five to seven.

Group size
Pairs.

What you need
Bean seeds, small plant pots with saucers, seedling compost, sand, sticky labels.

Science content
Plants need sunlight, carbon dioxide, water and nutrients to grow. Green plants are able to make their own food by a process called photosynthesis, where chlorophyll in the leaves helps to turn carbon dioxide, sunlight and water into a form of sugar and oxygen. Seedlings will sprout in the dark because they are using up the supply of food in the endosperm, but they will not grow very well and will be tall and spindly, eventually dying off.

What to do

Provide each pair of children with six pots, each with one bean – five planted in soil and one in sand. Place all the pots in sunlight except for one (with soil) which should be placed in a dark cupboard. Put sticky labels with the children's names on the pots. Water all the pots except one of the soil pots in the sunlight.

Allow the children time each day to check their pots and record what has happened by writing or drawing what they see. Explain that the pots should not be overwatered and that they must take special care of the plants in order for them to grow. Once they have sprouted, the children can also measure the height each day and compare their beans with other children's. They should record these results.

Ask the children to think of reasons why the beans have not all grown to be the same. Once the beans are very tall, the children can take them home to plant in the garden or if possible, plant them out at school so that they can watch the formation of flowers and beans.

Follow-up

• Make a display of other seeds using a wide variety of shapes, sizes and colours. Include pictures or real examples of what the seeds grow into.
• Compare the changes that take place with other living things such as tadpoles and baby animals. Do baby mammals always resemble their grown form? Do baby plants? Talk about how long things take to grow.
• Grow other plants in different ways, for example, from cuttings.

Sorting leaves

Age range

Six to eight.

Group size

Two to four.

What you need

A large number of different leaves of different shapes, sizes and colours, hand lenses, small hoops (optional), photocopiable page 121.

Science content

This activity will help develop skills for using identification keys. It will also show that plants, although similar, are not all the same and that even leaves on one plant can be different from each other. Leaves are classified into simple (single blades) and compound (several leaflets on a single leaf stem).

What to do

Provide each pair or group with lots of leaves. Ask them to look, touch and smell them to compare the sizes, shapes and colours. Point out the veins in the leaves and ask them to look at veins in all the leaves to find the differences. Discuss the texture of the leaves and whether some are shiny or dull. Encourage the children to use the hand lenses for a more detailed examination. Then ask them to sort the leaves in some way using their own criteria. The small hoops could be useful here to indicate sets. They could sort them into two groups first, then three, then four, ensuring they make more discerning choices each time. Discuss the sorting with the whole class to determine how many different ways were possible.

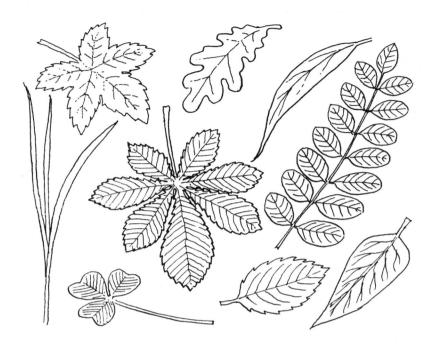

Next, provide each group with a copy of photocopiable page 121 and ask them to sort their leaves according to the key provided. Some children may be able to make their own keys, using a similar idea to the tree diagram.

Follow-up

Use pictures or objects for other sorting activities. Provide increasingly more difficult things to sort to encourage the children to look very closely at each object. Play sorting games – give each child a large picture of, for example, a pond creature and ask them to sort themselves into groups of creatures with the same characteristics. The development of these skills will make the use of identification keys in books more accessible to the children and will enable accurate identification when doing pond studies, for example.

Where would you find it?

Age range
Seven to nine.

Group size
Individuals.

What you need
Photocopiable page 122, a large sheet of paper, coloured crayons, scissors, adhesive.

Science content
The place where plants and animals live is called a habitat. Many living things are especially adapted to their habitat and cannot live elsewhere, while some are able to live in a greater variety of places. The survival of a living thing sometimes depends on its ability to change with changing circumstances and it is in this way that genetic changes take place over long periods of time.

What to do
Provide each child with a copy of photocopiable page 122 and ask them to look at the five different habitats represented. Ask them if they have seen any of these habitats and discuss what the conditions might be like in each – such as dry/wet, dark/light, how they might change over the seasons and so on.

Then ask the children to cut out all the pictures and group the living things according to the habitat in which they live. Explain that some things may be found in more than one area so for each one they will need to decide in which place they think it best belongs. Allow the children time to compare their sorted groups with others – is there a general agreement? If not, discuss the reasons why. Talk about how some things are especially adapted to where they live – a frog needs moisture and must lay eggs in water, ivy can cling to surfaces and grow up things, bees need wings to collect nectar and so on. Some children may like to draw other living things and sort these into the groups as well or you may like to add other things which are relevant to the area in which you live. The finished groupings can be stuck on large pieces of paper and put on display alongside pictures of other living things and their habitats.

Follow-up

Visit at least two examples of the five habitats and look closely at the plants and animals that live there. Consider such questions as: Do all pond creatures have similar features? Are the shapes of small flowers different from tall flowers? Do all minibeasts which live underground have smooth bodies? Are insects which live on trees camouflaged? Why do flowers have bright petals and strong smells? In what ways are water plants different from land plants? Do different plants grow in shady and sunny places? Such questions will help the children to look more closely at living things and will help them to discover some of the ways in which things have adapted to their environment.

Insect life cycle

Age range
Seven to eleven.

Group size
Small groups or whole class.

What you need
Mealworms (from pet shops), bran, a sponge, aquarium, apple, small pieces of wood, water, hand lenses, plastic Petri dishes or plastic lids, plastic spoons.

Science content
Mealworms are beetles which commonly live in wheat storage areas or in wood. They are excellent for showing children all of the stages in an insect's life cycle because they are so easy to maintain and, once established in an aquarium, can be viewed throughout their life cycle. Mealworms undergo metamorphosis whereby the larva (caterpillar stage) changes into a different shaped creature (the adult beetle). The life cycle stages are – egg, larva, pupa, adult.

What to do
Place a good layer of bran in the bottom of an aquarium for the mealworms to live in (and eat). Also put in a damp sponge, an apple core and some small pieces of wood. All that then needs to be done is to ensure the sponge is damp and the bran is topped up every few weeks. Allow some time to go by until you can see beetles, larvae and pupae in the bran and then you are ready for closer study working in small groups or the whole class.

Allow the children an opportunity to observe each stage of the life cycle (except eggs which are very difficult to

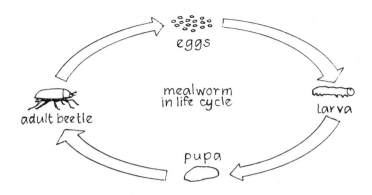

eggs

mealworm
in life cycle

larva

adult beetle

pupa

find). Using a plastic spoon, take out a mealworm larva and place it in a shallow dish with a small amount of bran. Ask the children to use a hand lens to observe the larva more closely. Encourage them to observe how it moves, how many legs it has, how many sections, what the eyes are like, how it eats and so on. Ask them to do a detailed drawing. They can also carefully measure the larva and conduct experiments to find out whether it can walk on smooth and rough surfaces and prefers the dark to the light.

Some of the pupae can be kept separately on a Petri dish as these do not need food or water. In this way the children may be lucky enough to watch the insect emerge. The young beetle is white and gradually turns black after moulting – encourage the children to look out for the different coloured beetles and moulted outer skins. The children could take it in turn to keep a daily diary of the whole family of mealworms – noting numbers of each stage seen, the sizes of adults, where each stage prefers to live and so on. Devise a rota so that each child has a turn at looking after the insects.

Follow-up
Study the life cycles of other animals such as frogs, chickens and mice and compare them with humans.

The function of plant parts

Age range
Nine to eleven.

Group size
Small groups or whole class.

What you need
A pencil, paper, pictures of plants (showing parts such as leaves, stem, flowers), a carrot, a knife, potted plants, some cut flowers, an assortment of leaves, a microscope (optional).

Science content
Flowering plants have specialised parts adapted for different purposes. The roots anchor the plant in the ground and absorb water and mineral salts for the rest of the plant. The stem supports the leaves and flowers and provides a passage for the vascular tubes which conduct water to all parts of the plant. The leaves are used to manufacture food by photosynthesis. They also give off water (transpiration) and allow the exchange of carbon dioxide and oxygen gases. The flowers contain the reproductive organs and, in some instances, attract insects for pollination. The fruit provides protection for the seeds. The seeds contain the embryo or unborn plant and a food store for the seed to use when it is in the soil. The vascular system consists of a series of tubes which conducts water and mineral salts upwards from the roots and carries dissolved food from the leaves to other parts of the plant.

What to do
Show the pictures of plants to the children and ask them to name the parts of the plant that they know. Can they also

suggest what the parts are used for? Look at a real potted plant and find the same parts on this as can be seen in the pictures.

Discuss the function of the root system with the children and use a carrot to demonstrate how roots are made. Ask them to point out the stem of the carrot. Which way up does it grow? How can they tell this? Look at the fibrous hairs growing out of the carrot. These are secondary roots and increase the surface area of the main or primary root so that more water and mineral salts can be absorbed by the plant.

Cut the carrot in half and observe the cross-sectional view. Then cut the carrot lengthwise. Look at the central core (this contains the vascular tubes). Is this different from the other parts of the carrot? Why?

Next, look at the stems of some cut flowers. How are the leaves arranged on the stem? Is there a pattern? Do different flowers have different leaf arrangements? Can you explain why? Observe other things about the stems such as their length, shape, colour, thickness and texture. Cut a stem in half and look at the interior. There is a hard outer part or epidermis and a softer inner part which fills the spaces between the vascular tubes and the epidermis. Discuss the functions of a stem.

Next, look at the arrangement of leaves on the potted plants. Observe the differences and similarities between the plants. How many leaves are there? Are they arranged so that they can all receive sunlight? Do the leaves vary in shape, colour and size? Can you tell which leaves are the newest? Are they simple (single leaf) or compound (many leaves)?

Use the collection of leaves to examine the leaf structure more carefully. How are the veins arranged? What is the purpose of the veins? Are some parts stronger or more 'woody' than others? Why? Slice a leaf into sections to look at the leaf parts more closely.

If a microscope is available, peel off a small piece of the lower part of a leaf to examine the leaf cells. Discuss the function of the leaves (follow-up with the next activity if desired).

Look at the parts of the flowers. Take a flower apart to look at the petals, stamens and pistil. Ask the children why they think a plant has flowers. (Follow-up with Flowering plant life cycle (page 33) if desired.) Ask the children to draw a flowering plant and label all the plant parts, saying what the function of each part is. Discuss their answers with the whole group.

Follow-up

How plants make food (opposite) and Flowering plant life cycle (page 33) make good follow-ups to this work. Also, grow cress seeds by lining a glass with blotting paper and placing the seeds between the paper and the edge of the glass. Keep the paper moist. This is a good way to look at roots growing. To show the function of the vascular system, place freshly cut celery stalks in coloured ink for a few hours to observe the lines of colour moving up the stem.

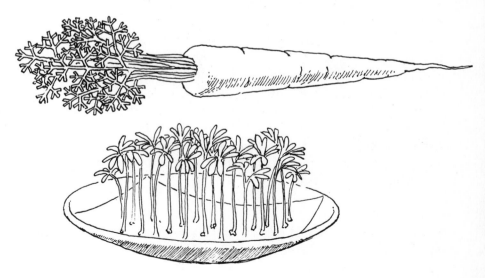

How plants make food

Age range
Nine to eleven.

Group size
Two to four.

What you need
A potted plant with variegated leaves (such as some geraniums), aluminium foil, iodine, water, methylated spirits, a small saucepan, a cooker, a glass jar.

Science content
Green plants are the only living things which can manufacture their own food. They do this by a process called photosynthesis. Green plants use sunlight, carbon dioxide, water and chlorophyll in their leaves to produce oxygen and food (starch). Chlorophyll is what makes the leaves green, thus in variegated leaves the part which is white does not contain chlorophyll. Testing leaves for starch is used to indicate whether or not photosynthesis has taken place.

What to do
Set up the following experiment to show that sunlight and chlorophyll are necessary for photosynthesis. Secure a piece of foil to both sides of one leaf on the potted plant. Place the plant in sunlight for several days. Then remove an uncovered leaf from the plant. Boil the leaf in water for a few seconds and place it in a glass jar with a solution of 70 per cent methylated spirits and 30 per cent water. (This should be done by the teacher.) Wash the leaf and then add a few drops of iodine. The green part of the leaf (the part with chlorophyll) will change colour and the white part (without chlorophyll) will not. Repeat this experiment with the foil-covered leaf, removing the foil first. The covered leaf should not change colour because it did not receive any sunlight to produce starch.

Ask the children to explain what the experiment shows. Why was it necessary to test an uncovered leaf as well as a covered leaf? Does this make it a fair test? Should we repeat the test to see if we get the same result? Should we try other kinds of plants?

Follow-up
Challenge the children to set up their own experiment to determine the requirements needed for plants to grow. Let them consider sunlight, amount of water, temperature, type of soil and so on. Encourage them to make an initial prediction of the outcomes first and then to record what actually happens.

Food chains

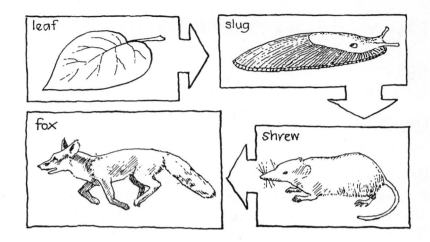

Age range
Nine to eleven.

Group size
Whole class.

What you need
Paper (A5), felt-tipped pens, safety pins, reference books on what animals eat. Using felt-tipped pens, write the names of the following plants and animals on the pieces of paper to serve as labels – wheat, field mouse, barn owl, microscopic algae, water flea, stickleback, perch, pike, human, grass, cow, leaf, slug, hedgehog, beetle, shrew and fox.

Science content
All animals ultimately derive their food from plants. Carnivorous animals eat other animals which eat smaller animals which eat plants. For example: pike eat perch, perch eat sticklebacks, sticklebacks eat water fleas and water fleas eat microscopic pond plants. This relationship is called a food chain. At the base of the chain there are usually numerous small plants and at the top there are a few large animals. If the population of one of the plants or animals in a food chain is altered, then all the others are affected.

What to do
Talk to the children about the meaning of a food chain and discuss several examples. Mention how all food chains eventually end with plants at the bottom and discuss how important it is to have plants in the environment. Talk about how pollution and human action can affect one element of the chain and the effects this may have on the other animals or plants in the chain. Ask the children to draw a food chain of their own choice, using well-known animals at the top, such as foxes or hedgehogs. Use reference books, if necessary, to find out what things eat.

When you think the children are familiar with the notion of food chains, pin each label on the back of a child and ask them to link hands with other animals or plants to make up a food chain. This activity will help the children to realise that humans are also a part of the chain and that some plants and animals form parts of many chains. Allow the rest of the class to have a turn at this activity. Do they get the same results?

Ask the children to write labels for other plants and animals on pieces of paper and to try out the activity again using different living things. This will help to reinforce how important plants are in every chain and how one living thing depends on others to survive.

Follow-up
Visit a pond or river. Write down food chains that are evident.

Flowering plant life cycle

Age range
Ten to eleven.

Group size
Two to four.

What you need
A variety of flowers, craft knives, cutting boards, hand lenses, a microscope (optional), pencil, paper, photocopiable page 123 (for follow-up activity).

Science content
The flower is the part of the plant which contains the reproductive organs (Figure 1). Most flowers have both female and male parts.

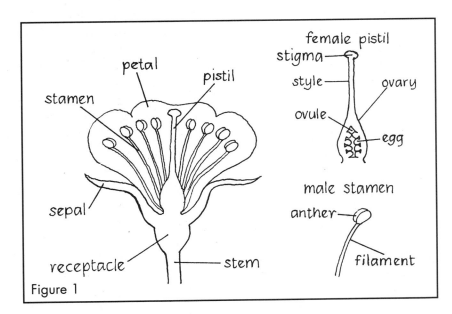

Figure 1

Pollination must take place before seeds can be produced. This is achieved when the pollen from one flower is transferred to another flower of the same species by insects and other animals and, sometimes, the wind. When the pollen lands on the stigma, it grows a tube into the ovary where the male cell and the female egg combine. The fertilised egg then grows into a seed. After fertilisation, the sepals, petals and stamens dry up, the petals and stamens fall off because they are no longer needed to attract insects, and the ovary develops into a fruit. Each fruit is specifically adapted for seed dispersal. Seeds which are very light or have wings (for example, dandelion, thistle, clematis) are dispersed by the wind. Some seeds have barbs which attach themselves to animals and are dispersed in that way; others are designed to split open suddenly, expelling the seeds some distance away from the parent plant. Some seeds are eaten by birds and are expelled in their droppings. Others are carried by water as a source of dispersal. Successful germination is determined by the required temperature, and the amount of water and oxygen necessary for that particular seed's growth.

What to do
Provide each group with an assortment of flowers and encourage them to look at the differences and similarities between them. Using hand lenses, the children can find out:
• what colours and shapes there are;
• whether the flowers have different smells;
• how many petals there are;
• whether the stem is textured, hairy, smooth or spiky;
• the shape of the leaves;
• how the petals feel;
• what the leaf veins are like.

Ask the children to make observational drawings of the full flowers, and separate leaves, stems and petals. Then, using flowers with a large base (receptacle), carefully cut one or two flowers open to examine what's inside. If the children are very careful, they will be able to cut open the ovary and see tiny eggs. If a microscope is available, let the children use this to obtain a much better view. The separate parts of the flowers could be attached to card for display and will keep for some time if covered with clear self-adhesive plastic.

Discuss with the children how pollination occurs and how seeds are made. If appropriate, comparisons can be made with human fertilisation. Ask the children how they think the seeds may be dispersed and discuss the role of animals, water and wind in dispersal.

Follow-up

Visit several different sites where flowers are growing. Encourage the children to make detailed observations and drawings at each site to compare the flowers growing in each place. A recording sheet such as photocopiable page 123 could be used for this purpose. Encourage the children to note:
• whether some flowers grow alone and others in groups;
• if there are flowers growing in shady places;
• whether flowers are different heights.
  See if they can work out why.
  Lastly, grow some flowers of your own at school from seed. You could experiment with different soil types and different conditions such as sunny, shady, cool, warm, with water, without water and so on. The children could predict which ones they think will grow best and then record the results.

DISPLAY IDEAS

• Cut out the shape of a large tree from card to mount on the wall. Add leaves with facts and figures about plants written on them.
• Make three-dimensional animal masks and mount them on the wall. Add information beneath each creature – preferred habitat, where it lives in the world, if endangered and why, and so on.
• Take photographs of plants and animals found in the locality and display them with the children's work arising from a wildlife walk.
• Make huge three-dimensional models of flowers out of card and label the plant parts.
• Make three-dimensional models of ideal habitats for certain animals or plants. Arrange them on a table beneath a wall display showing how to care for these living things.
• Paint a large pond – paint and cut out plants and animals which live in the pond and add them to the picture.
• Make a wall-hanging of plants and animals which live in a certain habitat.
• Draw pictures of plants and animals. Link them into food chains to make a wall display or mobile.
• Make three-dimensional models of insect life cycles and make a wall display using children's observational drawings and writing about them.
• Photograph bean seedlings as they grow. Display them with the children's reports about plant growth investigations.
• Turn a corner of the classroom into a rainforest. Hang paper vines, leaves, birds, plants and animals from the trees suspended on string.

Links with other curriculum areas

Art
• Animal masks.
• Clay modelling.
• Collages of forests/gardens/ponds.
• Making birds and their feathers from paper.
• Making mobiles.

Music
• Songs and rhymes to do with plants and animals.
• Making animal sounds.
• Animal/plant movement to music.

English
• Stories/poems about plants and animals.
• ABC of animals.
• Collective nouns of animals.
• Haiku poems.
• Debating issues such as zoos, use of animal products, rainforest decimation.
• Researching conservation projects.

Technology
• Designing and making homes for plants and animals.
• Posters – conservation, care of living things, endangered species.
• Designing a T-shirt – protect the rainforest, for example.
• Designing a wildlife area for your school.

Living things

Maths
• Surveys of favourite animals and graph the results.
• Facts and figures about living things – height of tallest tree, speed of fastest animal and so on.
• Fibonacci numbers.
• Patterns in nature.
• Leaf area, symmetry.

Geography
• Mapping local or school plants.
• Environmental issues – effects of human action.
• Mapping rainforests.
• Endangered species.

RE
• Stories of the Creation.
• Animals and plants in religion.
• Chinese New Year.
• Sacred animals.

History
• The use of plants and animals in history – transport, food, medicine.
• Myths and legends.
• Uses of plants and animals in ancient times, for example Egypt.

Water

This is a popular topic because it lends itself very well to cross-curricular activities. Water is vital to the existence of life on Earth and humans, animals and plants all make use of it in a variety of ways. Comparative studies of various water habitats will provide the children with an insight into some of these uses and will help to illustrate how living things are adapted to their particular environments.

A study of the properties and characteristics of water can lead to investigations into dissolving, evaporation, melting, freezing, sieving, filtering, buoyancy and reflections. The water cycle can also be studied and this may provide an opportunity to investigate the ways in which water can be harnessed as an energy source.

Uses of water

Age range
Five to seven.

Group size
Small groups or whole class.

What you need
Pictures of water sources – ponds, rivers, wells, seas, taps, rain, springs; pictures of water use – recreation, cooking, washing, industry, gardening; a collection of water samples – tap, pond, river, mineral water; paper, coloured crayons, plastic screw-top jars.

Science content
This activity will make the children aware of the wide variety of water sources and how water can be used. It will encourage close observation of different water samples so that children can detect similarities and differences.

What to do
Ask the children where water can be found and make a list of these places – puddles, rain, ponds, rivers, lakes, streams, seas, wells, springs, from a tap, bottled water and so on. Show them pictures of these water sources and ask the children to describe what the water looks like and how it behaves. This will lead on to talking about the uses of water – drinking, washing, cooking, recreation, industry and so on. Discuss pictures of these also. Talk about the fact that in nature there is salty as well as fresh water. Ask them to describe what water looks like after it has been used for washing-up, baths, cooking and so on. Invite the children to do some drawings of where water can be found and what it can be used for and display these with the other pictures.

Collect some different samples of water – tap, pond, river, bottled and put them in some plastic screw-top jars. Working with a small group, ask the children to look at each water sample and make comparisons between them – colour, transparency, amount of floating debris and so on. Can they think of reasons why the tap water is clear and the pond water is not? Ask them where they think the tap and the bottled water come from and how rivers and ponds fill up with water. (*Safety:* Warn the children not to taste any of the water samples and to wash their hands thoroughly after this activity.)

Follow-up
Take the children outside on a rainy day and ask them to look at how the water hits the ground, where it collects, what things can be found in puddles, how wet the grass/soil gets. If possible, visit different water sites so the children can observe the animals and plants that live in each place and perhaps the uses we make of them. (*Safety:* Very close supervision and many adult helpers will be needed with younger children when visiting water sites.)

Heating and cooling water

Age range
Five to seven.

Group size
Small groups or whole class.

What you need
Water, a measuring jug, an ice-cube tray, ice-cubes, saucers, two sponges, a paper towel, cotton wool, a kettle, a freezer.

Science content
Water is a liquid. It turns into a solid when you freeze it (0°C). To melt it, you need to use heat energy such as a warm room, your hand or by placing it in sunlight. Warmth causes the water to evaporate as water vapour into the air.

What to do
Set up the following, using equal amounts of measured water in two saucers for each one:
• water only;
• water in a sponge;
• water in cotton wool;
• water on a paper towel.
　Place one of each of the above near a source of heat, for example, near a radiator or in the sunshine. Place the other saucers in a cool, shady place.
　Ask the children to predict what might happen to the water in each case and to give a reason why. Allow them time to make periodic observations of the saucers and ask them to record this in some way. Can the children say what has happened to the water? Why has it disappeared? Has the water in the hot place gone more quickly? Why?

Discuss puddles and how quickly they dry up on a hot day compared to a cool day. Is there any difference in the rate of evaporation between the water only, paper towel, sponge and cotton wool saucers? Can the children offer reasons for this?

Demonstrate what happens to water when it is boiled by using a kettle. Do not allow the children to use the kettle or get too close. Let them watch the steam as it comes out of the spout. Where does it go? What happens to the water inside the kettle? Does the amount become less? Place a measured amount in the kettle, boil for a few minutes and then re-measure once the water has cooled. Is there less water? Explain that heating the water has caused it to evaporate into the air. Compare this with their own earlier experiments using the saucers of water.

Next, place some water in an ice-cube tray and place it in the freezer. Ask the children to tell you what will happen to the water. When frozen, take the cubes out of the tray and let the children touch the cubes. How do they feel? What has happened to the water? Why? Ask them to tell you how they could make the ice-cubes into water again. Try out their ideas to see if they are right or place the cubes on a saucer in a warm place and allow the children to observe what happens. Ask them to tell you why the ice has melted.

Follow-up
Compare water to other liquids such as fruit juice, shampoo and honey. Will these liquids also evaporate and freeze?

Float or sink?

Age range
Five to seven.

Group size
Two to four.

What you need
A bowl or bucket of water and assorted classroom objects such as a wooden peg, a marble, a plastic ruler, a piece of wood, paper-clips, a plastic spoon, a metal spoon, a glass jar, a foil tray.

Science content
Things float or sink due to their density in relation to water. Things which float are lighter or less dense than water. When an object is put into water, it pushes down on the water, but the water also pushes upwards. Things which are heavier or more dense than water push more strongly downwards and so they sink. Wood is less dense than water so it floats. *Lignum vitae* is the only wood which will sink because it is denser than water.

What to do
Provide a group of children with a container of water and the collection of objects. Ask them to look at each object, feel them and then predict whether they will float or sink. Ask them why they think this. They should then record their predictions by drawing or in writing.

Place each object into the water one at a time and let the children observe what happens. Some objects may float at first but will slowly sink (such as a wooden peg which has a metal clip). Try putting the objects into the water in different ways such as the ruler flat or the bottle upwards – does this alter how the objects behave? Why? Encourage the children to record what happens. Can they name materials which will always float or always sink? How do they know this? Relate what they have observed to water safety – what could you throw to someone in trouble in a pool that will help them to float?

Encourage the children to test out other objects of their own.

Follow-up

Give each child a piece of modelling clay of the same size. Ask them to make a boat and to see if it will float. This is harder than it appears and the children will need to experiment with different designs such as the height of the sides, the shape of the base and the thickness. They could draw each design they make and record whether it floated or not. Ask the children to decide what those that float have in common and relate this to real boats.

Water temperature

Age range
Seven to nine.

Group size
Small groups.

What you need
Water, a kettle, three bowls, a spirit thermometer.

Science content
Touch is not an accurate measure of hot or cold but a thermometer is. The upper fixed point of a thermometer is 100°C (the temperature of the steam above boiling water) and the lower fixed point is 0°C (the temperature of melting ice).

What to do
Prepare three bowls of water – one fairly hot, one tepid and one cold. Ask the children to take turns to put one hand in the hot water (make sure it is not too hot!) and one in the cold. After approximately one minute, put both hands in the tepid water. What does each child feel? Can they say how hot or cold the water feels to each hand? (The hand that was in cold water feels that the tepid water is warm and the hand that was in the hot water feels the tepid water to be cool.)

Ask the children how the water temperature could be measured more accurately. Show them a thermometer and explain in simple terms how it works. Let them practise reading the markings on it. Use the thermometer to measure the temperature of the hot, tepid and cold water. Help the children to read the thermometer correctly. How long does it take for the tepid water to reach the same temperature as

the cold water? How long does the hot water take to cool down? How could you make the cold water warmer? (Try placing it near a heater or in a sunny spot.) How could the hot water be cooled quickly? If possible, compare water temperatures of places outside such as ponds, streams, puddles and so on. Encourage the children to think of reasons why the temperatures are different.

Follow-up
Look at other types of thermometers such as clinical and liquid-crystal. Let the children measure their body temperature by placing liquid-crystal thermometers on their foreheads and clinical ones under their armpits. Ask them to measure air temperatures as part of weather recording in order to develop the skill of reading a thermometer correctly.

Pond study

Age range
Seven to eleven.

Group size
Small groups or whole class.

What you need
White plastic trays, plastic spoons, pond nets, magnispectors, plastic jars with lids, hand lenses, identification books, photocopiable page 124 (optional).

Science content
Ponds contain a wide variety of plant and animal life. They can be used to illustrate life cycles, habitat zones, food chains and seasonal influences. Observations of plants and animals in the pond can help children to understand how these living things are adapted to their environment.

What to do
Select a suitable pond site (permission may be needed for off-school sites) and make sure you have enough adult helpers to supervise the children. Before visiting the site, talk to the children about how they should behave – there are many outdoor study codes available but one produced by the children themselves will have more relevance. Consider such things as suitable clothing and footwear, replacing creatures after studying them, suitable noise levels, placing specimens in the shade, not leaving litter and so on. It is also very helpful to let the children become familiar with the equipment before venturing outside. Plastic spoons are useful for transferring small creatures, white trays help the children to see the creatures and a long-poled net will help to find bottom-dwelling plants and animals.

The following are a number of possible activities which can be carried out at the pond site:

• Sit quietly at the edge soon after arrival. What can you see and hear?

• Draw the shape of the pond and do a cross-section showing where plants are found.

• Collect samples of creatures and plants, then use identification keys to name them.

• Watch creatures in trays — how do they move, feed, breathe? Note the number of segments, legs, eyes, feelers and so on. Use photocopiable page 124.

• Collect samples from different areas of the pond — top, middle, bottom and compare the types of animals and plants found in each area. What do you notice?

• Make a diary of the changes throughout the year if the site is close enough.

• Look closely at the pond plants — methods of anchoring, leaf shapes, stem size and shape — and compare these to land plants, especially those in close proximity to the pond. How have pond plants adapted to their environment?

• Look for evidence of animal homes – caddis-fly larva cases, snail shells, holes in the bank and so on.

• Do some creatures only live near certain plants or at particular depths? How have pond creatures adapted to their environment? What evidence of reproduction can be found? Look for different egg samples.

It might be a good idea to consider pollution levels – the type and amount of certain creatures can be used as indicators:

Group 1: mayfly and stone fly nymphs – no pollution.

Group 2: no group 1 but freshwater shrimps and caddis-fly larva – slight pollution.

Group 3: no group 1 or 2 but water lice and bloodworms – medium pollution.

Group 4: no group 1, 2 or 3 but rat-tailed maggots and sludgeworms – heavy pollution.

Group 5: no creatures – very polluted.

Whatever the level of pollution, always ensure that the children wash their hands after visiting the pond.

Follow-up

Ask the children to compare the pond to another water site such as the sea-shore or a river. They can carry out similar studies and then consider the similarities and differences between them. Use photocopiable page 124 to make detailed studies of water creatures.

Aquarium study

Age range
Seven to eleven.

Group size
Two to four.

What you need
An aquarium, gravel (from pet shop), cold water plants (such as milfoil and pondweed), goldfish, a bucket, water, newspaper, goldfish food, photocopiable page 125.

Science content
Plants and animals are suited to their environment. There are life processes common to all animals, such as feeding, breathing, movement and reproduction.

What to do
Clean out the aquarium if necessary and wash the gravel by putting it in a bucket under running water. Place the gravel in the bottom of the aquarium and anchor the pondweed into it. Place a sheet of newspaper over the weed and gravel, then pour water into the tank. The paper will prevent any disturbance of the gravel. Remove when the aquarium is full.

Let the tank stand for a few days and then put in the goldfish. Encourage the children to observe the fish closely, noting how they move, breathe, feed and so on. Photocopiable page 125 can be used to give the children ideas on what to look for.

Ask the children to look for similarities and differences between the fish. What colours are they? Do they all have the same number of fins? Do they all eat the same things? Do they move in the same way? In what ways are fish different from humans and other animals? In what ways are they similar to humans?

Provide opportunities for all the children to care for the fish by arranging a rota system for feeding and cleaning.

Follow-up
Compare the fish in the class aquarium with fish in a freshwater stream or pond. What differences and similarities can be noted? Do these fish eat the same food? Move in the same way? In what ways is their behaviour different?

Hard or soft?

Age range
Nine to eleven.

Group size
Two to four.

What you need
Mineral water (still), distilled water, liquid soap or washing-up liquids, a pipette, two plastic bottles with screw-tops, a kettle, pieces of cotton cloth, two bowls or ice-cream containers, soil.

Science content
Water can be described as hard or soft. Hard water is water that will not lather easily. It contains minerals which have been dissolved from rocks or soil. Soft water contains little or no mineral matter in solution. Hard water can be made temporarily soft by boiling. Soft water can be made hard by dissolving Epsom salts in it.

What to do
Pour some distilled water into one bowl and some mineral water into the other. Ask the children to feel the water, look at it and perhaps smell it to see what differences they can observe. Then pour equal amounts of each type of water into two plastic bottles. Explain that some water is called 'hard' and some 'soft' and that they are going to find out how the type of water can affect the amount of suds produced by soaps.

Using a pipette, add equal amounts of liquid soap to each bottle and screw on the tops. Gently shake each bottle. Which water sample produces the most suds? Next, try to produce the same amount of suds in each bottle (say 2cm) by gradually adding drops of soap to fresh water samples. Which water needs the most soap to make the required amount of suds? How would this affect washing things in the home?

Test this out by using two small pieces of cotton cloth. Make them equally dirty by rubbing them in soil and place them into two bowls of water (one mineral, one distilled) with equal amounts of liquid soap in each. Stir the water to make suds. Leave the material to soak for two minutes then remove the two pieces and see what differences there are. Discuss the notion of a fair test – have the children considered all the variables? The same experiments could be tried after boiling the two types of water. Does this have an effect on the results?

Follow-up
Test different brands and types of soaps, powders and liquids. Which one seems to clean best? Do they do what they claim? Try different stains such as grass, oil and sauce in both types of water. Make predictions and record the results.

Solutions

Age range
Eight to eleven.

Group size
Two to four.

What you need
Water (hot and cold), salt, sugar, flour, sand, cooking oil, a teaspoon, coffee, clear plastic jars, coffee filters, nylon tights or fine netting, a selection of different fabrics, a measuring jug, saucers, a funnel.

Science content
A solution is a mixture of a solvent (such as water) and a solute (such as salt). Not all substances dissolve in water and some only partially dissolve. There is a limit to the mass of solid that can dissolve in water and this limit is different for different solids. Heating can increase the rate at which solids dissolve. Solids which have been dissolved can be recovered by evaporation. Insoluble solids can be separated from solutions by filtering.

What to do
Pour the same amount of cold water into six jars. Ask the children to predict what they think will happen if a teaspoon of each substance (salt, sugar, coffee, sand, flour and cooking oil) is placed into the six jars of water. Observe what does happen. Ask the children to think of ways to speed up the dissolving. Try stirring. What happens? Do all the substances dissolve? Why not? Try the experiment again using warm water. Record the results. Are the results the same? Do substances dissolve more quickly in warm water? Can the children suggest why?

Next, ask the children to keep spooning and stirring sand, sugar and salt into three separate jars to see how much of each will dissolve. Will the substance always dissolve? How many teaspoons of each does it take before the water can no longer dissolve the substance and it remains in the bottom of the jar?

Ask the children to suggest ways in which the dissolved substances could be separated from the water. Try evaporation. Place a small amount of salt solution in a saucer, then place the saucer in a sunny or warm position. Observe what happens. Where does the water go? What is left in the saucer? Can other dissolved substances be separated in the same way? Test this out.

Filtering is another way to separate mixtures. Allow the children to experiment with different filters such as coffee filters, nylon tights and different fabrics to see which one works the best. Mix some sand and water in a jar. Place a funnel in another jar and put a coffee filter paper in the funnel. Pour the water mixture into the funnel and make a note of how clear the water is as it filters through. What is left in the filter? Ask the children to predict how effective nylon tights will be as a filter then try this in the same way. Test different fabrics and compare the results. Record the results and compare the results of different groups. Do they reach the same conclusions? How accurate were their predictions?

Follow-up
Separate solids from mixtures by experimenting with sieves of different sizes.

Buoyancy

Age range
Nine to eleven.

Group size
Pairs.

What you need
Kitchen scales, a glass beaker or drinking glass, a small bottle such as a glass medicine bottle (with a lid) which floats, a washing-up bowl, water, a jug.

Science content
This activity will help to explain more fully why things float or sink in water and is a good follow-up to the Float or sink activity earlier in this section for older or more able children.

An object floats due to the upthrust of water acting upon it. This is called buoyancy. When an object is placed in water, it displaces some water making the water level rise. If the amount of water displaced equals or is less than the mass of the object itself, it floats. If the amount of water displaced is greater than the mass of the object, the object sinks.

What to do
Stand the scales in the washing-up bowl and remove the pan from the scales. Adjust the needle to zero. Place the glass container on the scales and fill it with water right to the brim so that it almost overflows. Record the weight.

Gently drop the medicine bottle (with its top screwed on) into the water. Some water will spill into the bowl. Remove the scales from the bowl and replace the pan on top. Readjust the needle to zero. Pour the water from the bowl into the pan and record how much this weighs. Then weigh the medicine bottle. The weight of the displaced water and the medicine bottle should be the same. Discuss the outcome with the children. Explain that this helps us to understand why things float or sink.

Fill the medicine bottle with water and replace the top. Conduct the experiment again. This time the bottle should sink. Does the displaced water weigh more than the bottle? Test other objects which float or sink. How do the results compare?

Follow-up

Find out how buoyancy is affected by salty water. Make a very salty solution of water in a glass beaker and float a Plasticine boat in it. How many paper-clips will it hold before it sinks? Try this with tap water and compare the results. Relate this to the Plimsoll line on ships.

The water cycle

Age range
Ten to eleven.

Group size
Whole class.

What you need
A kettle, water, a metal tray, paper, pencils.

Science content
Water is constantly moving in a cycle. It evaporates from the sea and other water masses, then condenses to form clouds which eventually drop rain on to the earth again. Figure 1 illustrates the cycle.

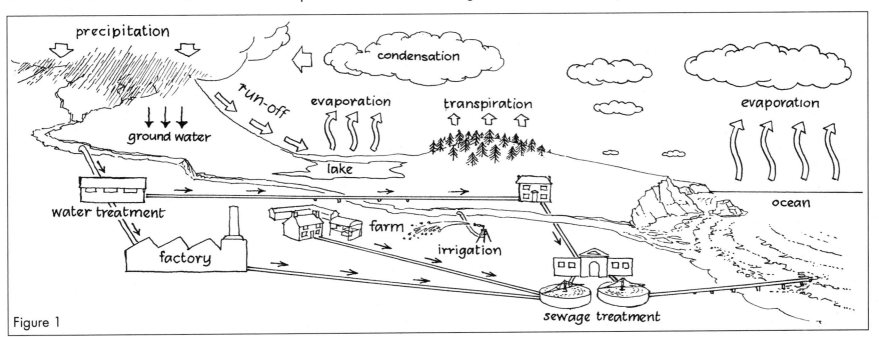

Figure 1

What to do

Ask the children what they think happens to the water that disappears down a sink. Where does it go to? What happens to it along the way? Ask them how rain is made and what happens to the rain once it hits the ground. Who/what uses the water? How can water be used by plants, animals, humans? How can water be polluted? What happens to this polluted water? Where do we get our drinking water from? Where do people in other countries get it from?

Talk to the children about the water cycle and how water is constantly moving from one place to another. Demonstrate how water evaporates and condenses by boiling a kettle and holding a metal tray above the jet of steam. What happens? Liken this to the formation of clouds and rainfall.

Provide the children with paper and pencils so that they can draw their own water cycle. Make sure they label the diagram. Tell them about aspects they may not think of such as transpiration from plants.

Follow-up

• Find out how water can be purified and re-used. Find out where your local water supply comes from and which authority is responsible for maintaining healthy levels. Visit a sewage treatment works or water treatment station.
• Conduct a survey of local water sites such as lakes, rivers and ponds. Are they polluted? If so, contact the local authority to find out how this can be rectified.

DISPLAY IDEAS

• Paint a picture of a fish tank or a cross-section of a pond. Ask the children to draw objects which would float or sink and fix these to the large picture. Display the finished picture alongside a tank of water and real objects to be tested out.
• Make mobiles of plants and animals which live in water. Dangle strips of blue crêpe paper around them to look like water.
• Make a collage of pond plants and animals.
• Make a mural showing all the uses of water.
• Display a collection of water samples in clear bottles – tap, mineral, distilled, pond, river, puddle, sea. Provide hand lenses for children to look at these closely. Add a background of pictures showing where we find water.
• Paint water scenes on the windows.
• Turn the book corner into a coastal cave with three-dimensional sea birds, seaweed, coastal animals and so on.
• Make a display of books or posters about water. Add question cards to encourage children to find out things.

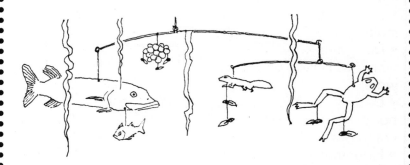

Links with other curriculum areas

Maths
- Capacity, volume.
- Measuring liquids.
- Area of ponds, measuring depth.
- Speed of river flow.
- Surveys – e.g. favourite seaside resort. Graph results.
- Weather measurements.
- Investigation – how many drops of water will this bucket hold?

RE
- Use of water – baptisms, holy water.
- Hindu – River Ganges.
- Judaism – Festival of Sukkot.
- Jonah and the whale.
- Noah's Ark.
- Jesus and the sea – disciples.
- The parting of the Red Sea.

Geography
- River systems – stages of a river.
- Coastal erosion and deposition.
- Weathering and erosion.
- Mapping regional or world rivers.
- Mapping seas and oceans.
- British fishing ports – location.
- World water supplies.

English
- Writing stories/ poems about rivers, the sea, ponds.
- Sending messages in a bottle.
- Water mythology – Neptune, mermaids.
- Writing water safety rules.
- Discussing water issues such as drought in Africa, pollution.
- Water ABC words.

Water

Technology
- Designing and making boats.
- Making a model lighthouse.
- Designing and making a water wheel.
- Designing a machine which will clean dirty water.
- Designing posters/ badges to tell people not to pollute water.
- Planning a menu for a fish restaurant.

History
- Famous sea voyages.
- The history of boats.
- Sea battles.
- Great civilisations on rivers, e.g. the Nile.
- The development of settlements due to water sources.
- Canal development.
- The history of steam power.

Music
- Making pitched instruments – filling bottles with water.
- Listening to sea songs/shanties.
- Making water sounds.
- Handel's *Water Music*.

Art
- Using washes in painting.
- Making 3-D fish.
- Making collage seascapes.
- Painting a pond mural.
- Painting windows with underwater scenes.
- Making tissue paper water scenes.
- Painting ships/boats.
- Painting reflections on water.

The study of air provides children with a variety of scientific investigations concerning the properties of air itself as well as wider aspects such as flight, sound and wind energy.

Although air cannot be seen, its effects can readily be investigated and children should be given the opportunity to explore air movement and pressure, the constituents of air and how air is used by living things, including human activities such as flying.

A topic on sound will enable the children to explore aspects such as vibrations, pitch and loudness, how sounds are heard and soundproofing.

What is air?

Age range
Five to seven.

Group size
Four to six.

What you need
A collection of solid objects – chalk, a book, building blocks, toys; liquids – milk, oil, water, honey; objects with air inside – inflated balloon, balls; extra balloons, a balloon pump, containers for the liquids.

Science content
Solids maintain a definite shape because their molecules stay in one position. The molecules in a liquid stay close together, but move about. The molecules in a gas move about very rapidly. We cannot see air but it takes up space, as demonstrated by balloons.

What to do
Display the collection of objects in groups. Ask the children to look at each group and say what differences there are between them. Allow them to feel the objects – do the solids change shape if squeezed? Pour the liquids from one container to another – notice how they take up the space. Let the children touch the liquids. What do they feel like?

Ask them what they think is inside the balls and balloons. Blow up a balloon yourself. Ask the children to say what is happening. Where does the air come from? What happens to the shape of the balloon? Let the balloon go and watch what happens. Why does this happen? Let the children use a balloon pump to blow up some balloons themselves and then let them go.

Ask the children to find solids, liquids and gases in their classroom and draw them (you may prefer to use terms such as 'hard', 'wet' and 'has air inside'). Add these drawings to the display of objects.

Follow-up
• Talk to the children about how we use air – hot air balloons, gliders, planes and so on.
• Make a simple kite and fly it.

Sounds around us

Age range
Five to seven.

Group size
Whole class together or in small groups.

What you need
Any classroom objects which make a noise such as – chalk on a board, a stapler, a tambourine, a tin of pins, a book opening and closing and so on; a large space or hall.

Science content
Sounds are caused by objects vibrating. The vibrations spread through the air to the ear and we hear them.

What to do
Ask the children to sit very still and quiet with their eyes closed. Ask them to listen quietly for a minute and try to remember all the sounds they can hear. Then ask them to tell the whole group what they could hear. Write down the sounds on a large piece of paper. Can sounds from outside or other rooms be heard? What was the loudest/softest sound? Do the children like or dislike some of the sounds? Why? This activity could be carried out at different times of the day to note any differences and similarities. Are some sounds constant? Less frequent? Very rare?

Next, ask the children to close their eyes while you move quietly around the room, stopping in different places to clap your hands. Can the children point in the direction of the sound? Try this several times. Are they always correct? Now make sounds with different objects to see if the children can guess the sound. They could also try this themselves with a partner who is blindfolded or has eyes shut.

Go to an area with a large space such as the hall. Tell the children to sit in a circle, then ask them to make a noise of their own – with their hands, mouth, feet. How many different sounds can the group make?

Then ask the children to sit with a partner and get them to make up their own sound. Ask one of each pair to stand and go to the other side of the room, standing with their backs to the others. Signal to one of the children sitting to make their sound. Can their partner recognise it? They can raise their hand if they do or, if you think they are capable, they could move slowly backwards until they reach their partner, following the sound all the time. If too many of the pairs have similar sounds, this will be difficult so encourage them to invent very different sounds like animals, birds, vehicles and so on. This game is fun and will help children to discriminate between sounds. As they get better at the game, two or three children could make their sound at the same time. Do all three of their partners respond?

Making sounds

Age range
Six to eight.

Group size
Two to four.

What you need
Tins, plastic containers with lids, beads, pasta, straws, blocks of wood, elastic bands, bottles, water, rulers, plastic combs, tissue paper, nails, a hammer, pictures of musical instruments.

Science content
Sounds are made when objects vibrate. We can make sounds by shaking, plucking, scraping, banging and blowing. Sounds can be soft or loud.

What to do
Demonstrate how sounds are caused by vibrations by holding a ruler on a table top with most of its length overhanging the edge. Flip the end of the ruler so it vibrates. Do a similar experiment with an elastic band – hold it taut and pluck it, then watch the vibrations and listen to the sound produced. Hammer some nails into a piece of wood then stretch some bands between the nails and pluck them. Pieces of stiff card can be placed under the bands, to act as a bridge, to change the sound. Relate this to how a guitar works.

   Ask the children to tell you other ways of making sounds. Strike two rulers together or a ruler on a tin. Ask the children what musical instrument works in this way. Tell them to rub two wooden blocks or their hands together and listen to the sounds made. Explain that a violinist rubs a

Follow-up
Conduct a sound survey of the neighbourhood. Go into the playground – what can be heard? Perhaps a portable tape recorder could be used. Walk to the outside gates of the school and into the local area. Compare the sounds heard. Where were the loudest sounds heard? What were they? Where were most sounds heard? Which sounds did the children like/not like? The children could record the sounds they heard in drawings or writing and could be encouraged to make predictions. Where do they think they will hear the loudest sounds? Where will the quietest spot be? Why?

bow on the violin strings to make sounds. Ask them how we make a whistle work – what other instruments do we blow? Show the children pictures of musical instruments and talk about their names and how we make them work.

Tell the children they are going to make their own instruments. Provide them with all the objects listed above and challenge them to make things which make a sound. Can they make loud and soft sounds with the same 'instrument'? Possibilities include: wrapping elastic bands around open boxes; putting beads in containers with lids; rubbing wooden blocks together; hitting tins; filling bottles with water and blowing across the top; blowing through straws; putting tissue paper across a comb then humming, and so on. Discuss with the class the variety of sounds the children made and how they produced them.

Follow-up

Show the children a collection of percussion instruments. Ask them how they think they would use the instrument to make a sound. Encourage them to predict which ones could make the loudest and softest sounds. Allow them time to explore the sounds which they can make to see if their predictions were correct. Use your music sessions to extend this further. Can they follow a pattern of sounds – you make a rhythm by clapping your hands and they try to repeat this and so on?

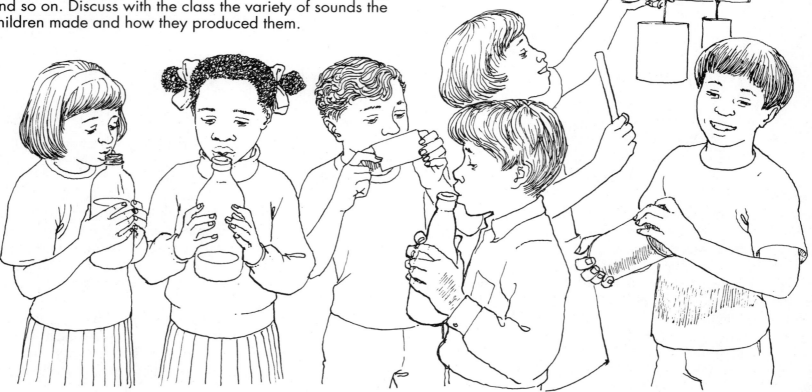

Changing sounds

Age range
Eight to eleven.

Group size
Two to four.

What you need
Eight empty milk bottles, water, a ruler, elastic bands of different thicknesses, nails, a hammer, a block of wood, a jug, some pitched musical instruments (optional).

Science content
Sounds have different pitches. Some are high and some are low. The faster something vibrates, the higher the pitch. When bottles are filled with water, the amount of water affects the sound made when you tap the bottle or blow across the neck. Air vibrates when you blow across the neck of the bottle, making sound waves. The unfilled portion of the bottle is called the resonating chamber and if this is small (the bottle is almost full), the vibrations are fast and the pitch is high. Large resonating chambers make low sounds. If elastic bands are plucked, thick bands will produce the lowest pitch.

What to do
Ask the children to fill each bottle with a different amount of water. Tell them to hit the sides of the bottles with a ruler and listen to the sounds made. Can they put the bottles in order from the lowest to the highest sound? Look at the levels of water in the bottles. What does this tell us about the sounds made? Ask them to blow across the tops of the bottles. Are the sounds the same as when the bottles are tapped? Are the bottles still arranged in order from lowest

to highest sound? Fine 'tuning' might be necessary by emptying or adding water so that the bottles sound very different from each other. Explain that the difference in sound is called pitch and, if possible, arrange for the children to listen to some instruments to demonstrate this.

Next, hammer six nails into a piece of wood and stretch some elastic bands of different thicknesses between them. Ask the children to pluck the bands and listen to the sounds. Do they also produce differences in pitch? What causes this?

Encourage the children to use these instruments or make their own to experiment further with pitch. Can they detect differences in the timbre (quality) of the sounds produced? Ask them to listen to some instruments to discover how the quality of the sound differs. Do some vibrate for longer? Are some sounds harsh or more pleasant? Can they explain to others why this is so?

Follow-up
• Make a class band using instruments the children have made themselves. Can they play simple songs? Perform a concert for other classes.
• Encourage the children to bring in instruments of their own and listen to the sounds made. Compare them to the sounds of the instruments they have made.
• Use records to listen to other instruments or attend a concert.

Soundproofing

Age range
Eight to ten.

Group size
Two to four.

What you need
Five shoe boxes, thin foam, carpet scraps, velvet or thick material, newspaper, adhesive, scissors, a battery, wire, a buzzer, a measuring tape. Optional – a larger box, egg cartons.

Science content
Sounds are made when objects vibrate. Sound can pass through some materials and not others. Some materials (such as soft fabrics, curtains and carpets) can absorb sound and are used for soundproofing purposes in buildings.

What to do
Make a small hole in one end of each shoe box. Line all the sides, including the lid, of four of the boxes with a different material. Make sure the lid still fits snugly on to the box.

Explain to the children that they are going to test out which material would provide the best soundproofing if a buzzer was sounding inside the box. Ask them to predict which material will work best and why.

Attach some wires to both terminals of a buzzer and place the buzzer inside the shoe box without any lining. Push the wires through the hole in the side of the box and attach the wires to the battery. (Ensure the children are aware that the buzzer will only work with the wires attached to the correct ends of the battery. Allow them some

time to experiment with the buzzer before placing it inside the box.) Listen to the sound of the buzzer with the lid closed. How loud is it? The loudness could be measured by recording the distance a child has to move away from the box before they can no longer hear the sound.

Then try the buzzer inside the other boxes and record the results. Compare the results of each material with the unlined box. Which material provides the best soundproofing? Why? When would the use of soundproofing be important or necessary? The children could use other materials of their own choice to line other boxes. A larger box might be needed to test egg cartons which provide a very good soundproofing material.

Follow-up
Investigate whether or not pitch has an effect on how easily a sound is heard. Make sounds of different pitches from behind a closed door or in another part of the room. Which sound can be heard the best – high or low pitch? Does this vary for different people? Can the children suggest why? Would this have an effect on the choice of sound for a car or fire alarm?

Properties of air

Age range
Seven to nine.

Group size
Two to four.

What you need
A metre ruler, two balloons, string, a pin, a balloon pump, two drinking glasses, a cork, a washing-up bowl, water, a football or basketball, electronic scales, a ball pump.

Science content
Air has no shape and cannot be seen but it takes up space and has weight of its own. When air is forced into a smaller space, such as inside a balloon, the air can be weighed by comparing the weights of the inflated and deflated balloon.

What to do
Blow up two balloons and attach them to each end of the metre ruler. Tie some string round the middle of the ruler and hang it so that the ruler is suspended. Adjust the position of the string on the ruler so that the balloons are balanced like a balance scale.

Ask the children to predict what will happen to the balance when one of the balloons is popped. Can they give reasons for their predictions? Pop one balloon and watch the results. What does this tell us about air? The children can draw the balance and show what happens before and after the balloon is popped.

Next, squeeze as much air as possible out of a football. Weigh the ball and record the weight. Pump up the ball and weigh it again. The difference will be quite small so good scales are necessary.

To show that air takes up space, half fill a bowl with water and float a cork on it. Place an empty glass upside-down over the cork and lower the glass into the water until the rim touches the bottom of the bowl. What happens to the water level inside it? Watch the cork for any sign of a change in water level. Now tilt the glass. Air bubbles will be seen rising to the surface. What happens to the water level in the glass now? Why?

Add more water to the bowl and place one glass into the water so that it fills up with water. Hold it upside-down in the water with one hand. With the other hand, lower

another empty glass (upside-down) into the water, tilting it under the first glass so that bubbles of air escape. Observe what happens to the water level in both glasses.

Follow-up

A study of air pressure follows on very well from this and two very simple demonstrations of air pressure for younger children are:
• Fill a glass to the brim with water. Place a piece of thin card tightly over the rim of the glass and quickly turn it upside-down. If you take your hand away, the card will stay in place because air pressure holds it up against the glass.
• Put your finger over a drinking straw filled with water. The water stays inside the straw. Remove the finger and the air presses on the water and it comes out of the straw.

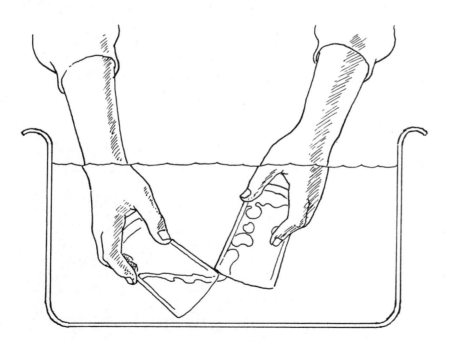

Air pressure

Age range
Nine to eleven.

Group size
Two to four.

What you need
A strip of paper (about 4cm x 20cm), a piece of A4 paper cut in half, a piece of stiff card folded to make a tunnel shape as shown in Figure 1, a hair drier, cotton, Blu-Tack, two ping-pong balls, a piece of dowelling or a long pencil, two milk bottles.

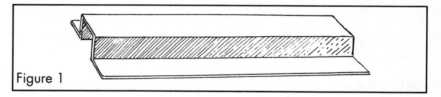

Figure 1

Science content
Air constantly exerts pressure. Flowing air exerts less pressure than stationary air (called the Bernoulli Effect). As a plane moves forward air passes over the top and bottom of the wings. The air has to travel a greater distance on top than underneath so the air moves faster, causing the pressure to drop. The pressure under the wing is greater than that above it, so the wings (and plane) are pushed upwards.

This can be demonstrated by blowing across a strip of paper. The passage of air causes the pressure to be less on top than underneath the paper so the greater pressure from beneath pushes the paper upwards. Blowing between two pieces of paper or between two suspended balls, causes

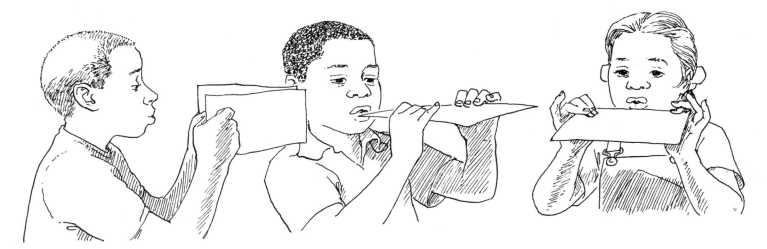

them to move together. This is because moving air has lower pressure than the surrounding air, causing greater pressure on the objects from the outside, pushing them together.

Blowing through the card tunnel causes the air pressure underneath to be less than the surrounding air. The greater pressure surrounding the card pushes down on it and keeps it in place.

What to do

Ask the children to predict what will happen to a strip of paper if they place its edge in front of their mouth and blow. Tell them to try it out and observe what happens. Can they predict what might happen if two pieces of paper (half A4) are held apart (about 3cm) and they blow down between them? Can they explain what is happening?

The same will happen if two ping-pong balls are attached to some cotton with Blu-Tack and are suspended from a piece of dowelling balanced across the tops of two milk bottles. Tell the children to use a hair drier to blow air between the two balls. What happens? Is this what was predicted?

Next, use the folded piece of card (Figure 1). Place it near the edge of a table and ask the children to blow through the gap and observe what happens. Can they lift it off the table by blowing? Can they say why not?

Explain that these experiments show that air can push down on things (pressure) from all sides and that when the push is greater on one side than another, the object will move towards the area of less pressure.

Follow-up

A study of how planes fly will demonstrate the practical uses of the effects of air pressure. Look at wing shape and uplift, propellers and jet planes.

Propellers

Age range
Nine to eleven.

Group size
Two to four.

What you need
Lengths of stiff wire or florist's wire, small beads, adhesive tape, card, scissors, plastic toy propeller, pictures of planes with propellers.

Science content
A propeller is designed so that when it is rotated it produces a force which pulls an aeroplane through the air. It helps the plane to develop lift, thereby keeping it up in the air. Propeller blades are set at an angle so that they can cut the air, pushing it backwards, which in turn pushes the plane fowards.

What to do
Show the children the pictures of planes with propellers. Ask them to tell you how they think the propeller helps the plane to fly. Show them the toy propeller and look at its shape. How does it compare with the ones in the pictures?

Explain to the children that they are going to make some propellers to find out which shape is best for cutting through the air. They could begin by making the propeller on this page.

Draw a blade like the one shown in Figure 1 on card. Cut along the solid lines and fold along the dotted lines. Attach the propeller to the wire using beads, making sure it can move freely. Ask the children to blow on the propeller to see how it moves.

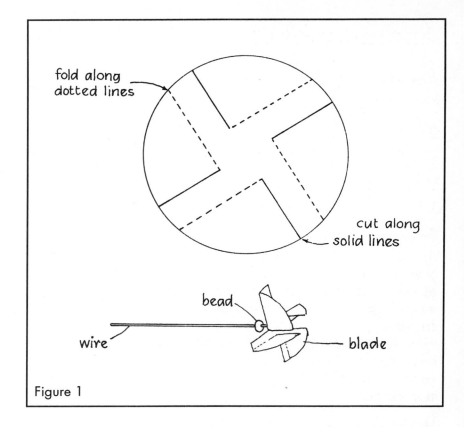

Figure 1

Next, ask them to design other differently-shaped propellers from card and attach these to wire also. How can they test out the propellers to see which one is 'best'? Allow the children time to devise their own tests. Discuss the results of each group's work. Did they try to make their test fair? How did they do this and how were the results recorded? Which group seemed to obtain the most accurate results? How was this achieved?

Follow-up
Make a model plane or hovercraft which uses propeller power.

Aerodynamics

Age range
Nine to eleven.

Group size
Two to four.

What you need
A4 paper, scissors, paper-clips, adhesive tape.

Science content
Aerodynamics is the study of airflow over moving objects. It is especially concerned with the streamlining of cars and planes to reduce air resistance or 'drag'. An aerofoil is a wing-shape that cuts through the air in such a way as to create lift. The lift is created because the air passing over the top of the wing moves faster than the air below because it has further to go. This creates low pressure above the wing. As air always moves from high to low pressure, it causes the wing to lift.

What to do
Ask the children to make a paper plane of their own design. Allow them to test the plane to see how well it flies. Then ask them to make another plane with a different wing shape and compare the performance of this plane with the first one. Ask them to make several more planes with different wing shapes – they may need to use paper-clips or adhesive tape to make their planes more stable. Some alternative designs can be seen in Figure 1.

Can the children devise a fair test to find out which plane flies the best and why? They will need to consider points such as how they throw the plane each time, how many times they test each plane, how do they determine the 'best' plane? Is it the one which flies the furthest? Straightest? For the longest time? They could record their results in some way and should be encouraged to draw each plane type to show the wing shape.

After each group has completed its investigation, bring the whole class together to compare results. Which wing shape appears to fly the best? Can they suggest why? Does the nose shape also have an effect? Why? Which was the best way to throw the planes? How did each group decide what was 'best'? Discuss how a plane achieves lift and what 'aerodynamic' means. Relate this knowledge to car shapes. Can the children see how this can affect fuel consumption and why most modern cars are similar shapes?

Follow-up
Make kites of different designs and investigate the best flying shapes and materials.

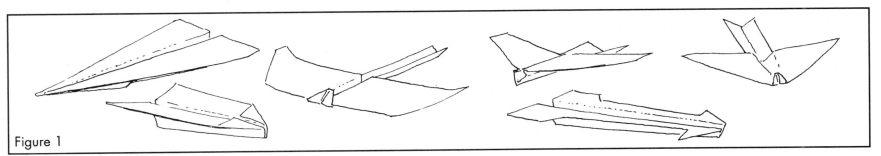

Figure 1

Air resistance and gravity

Age range
Ten to eleven.

Group size
Two to four.

What you need
Paper, two objects of the same size and shape but different weight (for example, a ping-pong ball and golf ball), a metal tray, a chair, string, scissors, cloth, a plastic bag, adhesive tape, kitchen scales, a set of plastic weights.

Science content
Gravity is the force which pulls objects towards the centre of the Earth. Objects of the same size and shape will fall at the same rate, even if they do not weigh the same. Air resistance is a force exerted upwards on the object as it falls. The greater the surface area of the object, the greater the air resistance and the slower it will fall.

What to do
Provide the children with the two balls and ask them to weigh them. Explain that they are going to drop the balls on to a metal tray to see which one hits the tray first. They need to drop the balls from the same height and at the same time while standing on a chair. Can they predict which one will land first and give a reason why? How can they ensure the test is fair? Encourage them to talk about this before doing the experiment. How many times should they test the balls? (The metal tray is used so that they can listen for the impact – if they hear two sounds, then one has hit before the other.)

Next ask them to drop a flat sheet of paper and a crumpled piece of paper of the same size and weight.

Which one lands first? Can the children suggest why? Compare the results of both tests. Can the children suggest why the balls landed together but the paper did not?

Talk to the children about gravity. Do they know what it is? Use the term air resistance when discussing the results of the paper test. Discuss how the results might be different on the moon and encourage the children to provide reasons why this might happen.

Ask them to investigate air resistance further by making a parachute using a piece of paper with a piece of string attached to each corner. Tie the string to a plastic weight then throw the parachute up into the air and watch how it descends. Experiment with different lengths of string, types of material for the canopy (cloth, plastic) and sizes and shapes of canopy to determine which offers the most resistance and provides the smoothest fall.

Follow-up
Find out more about gravity such as geotropism (how plants react to gravity), how astronauts cope without its effects and finding the centre of gravity of objects.

DISPLAY IDEAS
- Make models or mobiles of things which live in or use the air. Hang these on string from the ceiling.
- Paint a mural of animals which fly or glide.
- Make a display of paper planes, parachutes and kites which the children have made themselves. Add the children's writing and drawings of their investigations of these objects to the display.
- Make a music corner where children can experiment with making different sounds. Include posters of musical instruments.
- Collect objects with air inside them – balloons, balls and so on. Let the children use the collection for investigations and add objects of their own.

Links with other curriculum areas

Geography
- Map airports, air routes.
- Weather and climate.
- Satellite photographs.
- Aerial photographs.
- Air pollution.
- Holiday destinations.

Art
- Murals of things which fly.
- Bird masks.
- Sketching birds/planes.
- Decorating home-made musical instruments.
- Weather pictures.
- Blowing through straws on ink, thin paint.

History
- Myths and legends – Icarus.
- History of air travel.
- Air battles – e.g. Battle of Britain.
- Immigration.
- History of local airports.

English
- Stories and poems about flight, weather.
- Listing things which use air.
- Making word searches/crossword puzzles.
- Write newspaper reports on air disasters – plane crashes, tornadoes, hurricanes.
- Discuss air pollution.

Technology
- Design and make an instrument to measure wind speed.
- Make a model plane, hot air balloon, glider.
- Design posters to tell people how to prevent air pollution.
- Design a city on the moon – how will oxygen be made?
- Design a new plane/airport.

Air

Music
- Listening to songs about flight, air.
- Making own instruments – changing pitch.
- Finding out about wind instruments.

Maths
- Survey number of people who have flown on a plane – graph.
- Weather recording – make chart.
- Temperature reading.
- Distances – air travel.

RE
- Where is Heaven?
- Wind – Pentecost.
- Indian custom – Basant people – fly kites.

Planet Earth

This topic has close links with geography and many of the activities in this chapter could form the basis for a series of cross-curricular activities.

The earth provides us with a wide variety of different materials which have different properties and uses. Some of these materials are used in their natural state and some are processed by humans to form new materials.

A study of rocks and soils in the local environment can provide the children with experience in investigating similarities and differences, sorting and grouping and observation of characteristics such as appearance, texture and permeability. A study of rocks can also include investigations of metals and magnetism.

The earth provides us with many sources of energy. Some of these are natural, such as wind, waves and fossil fuels. Others can be manufactured by humans. A study of energy can give the children an understanding of how these resources help provide us with energy and what they can be used for.

Sorting materials

Age range
Five to seven.

Group size
Four to six.

What you need
A collection of natural and manufactured materials with common characteristics, for example: hard – rock, metal bar; soft – sheep's wool, rubber foam; grainy – sand, sugar; liquid – water, a soft drink; shiny – shiny leaf, metal foil; rough – bark, sandpaper; smooth – smooth leaf, cloth; straight/long – a stick, a ruler. Also old magazines, adhesive, paper, scissors.

Science content
This activity will give the children experience in observing, describing, sorting, identifying similarities and differences and the identification of natural and manufactured materials.

What to do
Provide the group with the collection of objects and allow them time to look at and touch them. Ask them to describe their colour, shape, texture and size. Encourage them to consider what each object is used for, then ask them to group the objects in some way of their own choosing – by colour, texture, use and so on. Can other children guess the criteria used for the grouping? Can the objects be grouped in another way? The children could draw the items in each group as a record of their sorting.

Encourage the children to consider which things they would find in nature and which things they think have been made by humans. If appropriate to the group, ask how they think some of these things are made – cloth, for example. The group could then cut out magazine pictures of things found naturally and things made by humans. These could be mounted on paper to form a display together with their own drawings of the objects. The children could also collect other objects – natural and manufactured – to add to a three-dimensional display.

Follow-up
Using the same collection of objects, ask the children to find out more about the properties of the objects, for example, which ones stretch, which ones bend, which ones twist. Do any dissolve in water? How can their shape be changed? Which ones change shape permanently and which ones return to their original shape? Which one is the strongest?

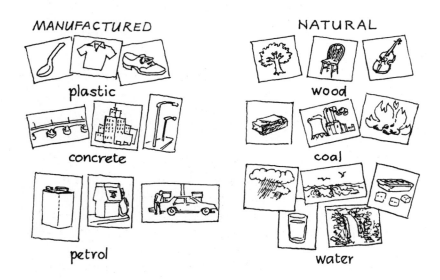

MATERIALS

MANUFACTURED
plastic
concrete
petrol

NATURAL
wood
coal
water

Heating and cooling materials

Age range
Five to seven.

Group size
Two to four.

What you need
Water, ice-cubes, a small saucepan, a cooker, chocolate, matches, a saucer, a craft knife, a freezer, an ice-tray.

Science content
Heating and cooling can bring about changes in materials. In a physical change no new substance is formed or destroyed, there is no change in weight and the change can usually be reversed easily (freezing/thawing water). In a chemical change the substance is changed and new substances are formed, there is a change in weight and a reverse change is difficult (burning a match).

What to do
Ask the children to predict what might happen if some ice-cubes were placed on a saucer and left to stand. Let them observe what happens and ask them to tell you why they think the ice melts. If they think light is the cause, leave the saucer in a dark place and observe again. Ask them how they think they could speed up or slow down the melting.

Next, place some water in an ice-tray in the freezer and some water in a saucepan on a heated plate. Ask the children to predict what might happen to the water in each case. Ask them whether they think ice is still water. What happens to the water when it is heated in the saucepan? Why does the amount of water get less? Where does it go?

Try using chocolate next. Ask them to predict what might happen if this is heated. Is it still chocolate when melted? How can it be made solid again?

Cut a matchstick in two with a craft knife. What has happened? Is the matchstick still wood? Now light another match and place it in a saucer. Let the children observe what happens to the wood. (Adult supervision is needed for this activity.) When it has cooled, allow them to feel the remains – is it still wood? Could this be made back into wood in some way? Explain that some things change forever when heated.

Follow-up

Reinforce the ideas presented here through cooking activities – make flavoured ice-lollies from fruit juice and bake some cakes or bread.

Uses of materials

Age range
Six to seven.

Group size
Four to six.

What you need
A collection of wooden things such as a tree branch, a log of wood, different types of timber, a spoon, a toy, jewellery, a bowl, a handle, a chair and so on. Pictures of things made from wood such as houses, furniture and so on.

Science content
Many common types of material are found naturally and can be used for a wide variety of purposes. Materials are chosen for a particular purpose according to the properties that make them suitable.

What to do
Show the collection of wooden objects to the children. Let them feel them. Encourage them to describe what they look and feel like. Talk about the texture, grain, colour, smell and hardness. Ask them to tell you something that all the objects have in common.

Do the children know where wood comes from? Which one of the objects shows them what wood looks like in nature? Ask them to tell you how they think the wooden spoon may have been made. What is it used for? Repeat these questions for the other objects. Can they suggest why wood has been used for these things and not another material? Could they all be made from rock, for example? Why or why not?

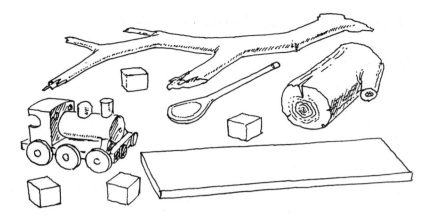

Look at the pictures. What things can they see that are made from wood? Why do they think wood was used? Could something else have been used instead? Look around the classroom. Ask each child to name something which has been made from wood.

Discuss all the uses of wood. Mention burning wood for heating if the children do not suggest this themselves. Discuss the hardness and thickness of different pieces of wood. Explain that very thin wood can be used to cover tables (veneers) whereas some wood is strong enough for doors. Some woods are good for carving and others are good for boat building and so on.

Finally, ask the children to record their findings in some way. Perhaps they could draw pictures of all the different uses of wood. They could also bring along their own wooden objects to add to a class collection.

Follow-up

Provide the children with a selection of woods, some thin, some thick, some hard, some soft. Encourage them to investigate the collection in some way. Do they all float? Can they be scratched with a fingernail? A nail? How easy is it to hammer a nail into the wood? Will any pieces bend?

Rocks and soil

Age range
Six to eight.

Group size
Four to six.

What you need
A collection of different rocks and soils, pictures of rocks and soil in the environment – cliffs, ploughing a field, pebbly beaches and so on.

Science content
This activity will provide the children with experience in observing, describing, sorting, finding similarities and differences and drawing. It should also provide an insight into the variety of rocks and soils and where they might be found.

What to do
Provide the group with a collection of rocks and invite them to describe them – colour, size, shape, texture, weight, smell, how brittle, how strong and so on. Ask them to group the rocks according to their own criteria and to record their grouping by drawing them. Can others guess the criteria used for the grouping? Discuss with others how else the rocks may be grouped.

Then ask the children to select one of the rocks and to find out more about it. They can draw it in detail and then write (or you can act as a scribe) a description of it. Encourage them to consider things such as: how heavy it feels; whether it has holes in it; whether it is made up of different colours and sizes of grains; whether you can scratch it with your fingernail. Other children can be asked to identify the rock by looking at the picture and description.

Next, ask the group to look at a collection of different soils to find similarities and differences between them. Allow them to feel and smell the soils. Can they find leaf matter or small pebbles in the soil? They could try to match the colour of the soil with crayons or paints.

Show the children pictures of places where rocks and soils can easily be seen. Ask them if they have visited any such places. Do they know what we can use rocks and soil for (such as building things and growing things)? Ask them to bring in samples of rocks and soils from their own gardens to compare with the class collection.

Follow-up

Conduct a survey of the rocks and soil in the school grounds or a neighbouring field/park. Take small samples in different places to compare the rocks and soils found there. If possible, use a spade to dig a deep hole and look at the layers of soil – note the differences in colour, texture and amount of moisture. Make rubbings or take photographs of rocks rather than take away large samples. Compare the rocks and soils found here with the class and children's own collections. What reasons can the children suggest for the differences/similarities?

Metals and magnetism

Age range
Six to eight.

Group size
Two to four.

What you need
Magnets – bar and horseshoe; a collection of different metals – steel, iron, aluminium, brass, copper; a collection of everyday things such as coins, a ruler, pins, paper-clips, metal foil, a glass jar, a nail, bottle tops, plastic lids.

Science content
Magnets have several properties – each magnet has two specific ends or poles; like poles repel each other, opposite poles attract; magnets attract iron, nickel, cobalt and alloys of these (for example, steel), they do not attract all metallic things; magnets are surrounded by a magnetic field.

What to do
Provide each child with a magnet and ask them to investigate which objects in the classroom are attracted to the magnet and which ones are not. Ask them to draw or write lists to show the results. Then provide them with a collection of everyday objects and ask them to predict which ones will be attracted to the magnet. Ask them to record their predictions and the results in some way. Did they find that all metallic things are attracted? Which were not? Use the collection of metals to show which ones are not attracted to the magnet.

Will the magnet still attract things through other objects? For example, ask them to try to attract a paper-clip through things such as a plastic lid, a thin piece of wood, a thin

book, metal foil, inside a glass jar, and so on. Ask them to predict what will happen first then record their results. Are some magnets stronger than others? Encourage them to try the same experiment with different sized and shaped magnets. Record what happens.

Follow-up
Challenge the children to think of uses for magnets and perhaps they could make a game using magnets.

Solids, liquids and gases

Age range
Eight to eleven.

Group size
Two to four.

What you need
A collection of solids such as – wood, a candle (wax), a nail, a ruler, butter, chocolate, salt, paper; a collection of liquids – water, a fizzy soft drink, honey, ketchup, milk; a blown-up balloon, baking powder, a spoon, vinegar, a jar, a glass.

Science content
The molecules in a solid stay in one position, hence solids can maintain a definite shape. The molecules in a liquid stay close together, but move about. The molecules in a gas move about very rapidly and rebound from one another. Applying heat causes molecules to move faster, hence a solid can be turned into a liquid and liquid into gas.

What to do
Provide the group with a collection of solid objects. Ask them to look at and touch each object to determine what they all have in common. Introduce the term 'solid' to explain that these objects are 'hard', they usually retain their shape even if moved or touched.

Ask them to compare the solids to the collection of liquids – what are the differences between them? Can solids be poured? Do liquids easily change shape? Compare the differences between the liquids. Are some easier to pour than others? Are some thicker? Do they all feel the same?

Finally, look at gases. Ask the children what is inside an inflated balloon. Explain that air is made up of different things called gases, such as oxygen and carbon dioxide. Pour some soft fizzy drink into a glass. What do the children notice? What are the bubbles made of? Add some vinegar to a teaspoonful of baking powder in a jar. Observe what happens (vinegar reacts with the baking powder to form carbon dioxide).

Ask the group to write down the differences between solids, liquids and gases. Do they all agree? Ask them to make a list of solids, liquids and gases in the classroom/home and compare their list with those of other groups in the class.

Follow-up

Experiment with changing solids, liquids and gases. Freeze liquids such as water and fruit juice. What happens? Melt some solids such as ice, chocolate or butter. Have the substances changed in some way? Boil some water in a kettle and observe the water vapour escaping.

Properties of soil

Age range

Nine to eleven.

Group size

Two to four.

What you need

Tin cans with both ends removed, glass jars with lids, water, a collection of different types of soil and sand, a washing-up bowl, a measuring jug, a stopwatch, a microscope (optional).

Science content

Soils vary greatly in texture, appearance and permeability. Permeability describes the ease with which water can pass through the soil. Water draining through soil plays several roles – it dissolves minerals for plants to use; it carries oxygen and carbon dioxide which help in the chemical decomposition of rock particles and it provides plant roots and soil creatures with oxygen necessary for respiration.

What to do

Invite the children to look closely at the different soils. What differences and similarities can they see? Encourage them to consider colour, texture, size of particles, how crumbly it is and so on. Can they suggest which soils would be best for plants and why? Explain that many plants need soil in which the water does not drain away too quickly and that soils vary in the amount of water they retain or allow to seep through. Explain that soils which allow water to pass through easily are called permeable. Tell them they are going to carry out an experiment to find out how permeable the soil samples are.

Stand a tin with both ends removed in a washing-up bowl. Fill it with soil to about 2cm from the top. Pour a measured amount of water into the tin and time how long it takes for the water to soak into the soil. As the water sinks in, encourage the children to watch what happens to the soil. Bubbles of air could appear. Discuss what this means and how the water helps to aerate the soil.

Do this with all the soil samples and compare results. Can the children provide reasons for different rates of water absorption between the different soils? What implications does this have for farmers and gardeners, for example? What effect would rain have when falling on an already waterlogged soil?

To find out about the constituents of soil, put a handful in a jar which is more than half-filled with water. Put on the lid and shake the jar vigorously until the soil and the water are thoroughly mixed. Leave it to stand for 24 hours and the soil should settle into layers – the heaviest, usually sand, on the bottom and the lightest layer on the top (often decayed plant and animal matter). Encourage the children to think about how the soil came to be made up of these layers. Use a microscope to examine soil particles more closely.

Follow-up

The first activity can also be carried out in the local area. The tins can be pushed into the ground and the permeability rates of different soils in different locations can be compared. How does this affect the types of plants growing there?

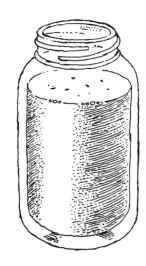 

Properties of rocks

Age range
Nine to eleven.

Group size
Two to four.

What you need
A collection of rocks, such as: igneous – granite, basalt, pumice, obsidian; sedimentary – sandstone, limestone, conglomerate, shale; metamorphic – marble, slate, gneiss, schist; hand lenses, a coin, a compass, paper, a pencil, reference books for identification.

Science content
Rocks are made up of minerals which are usually found in the form of grains or particles. The size and arrangement of mineral grains help to identify rocks. Rocks can be igneous,

sedimentary or metamorphic. Igneous rocks have been formed from cooled and hardened magma which comes from deep inside the earth and is sometimes thrown out of volcanoes when they erupt. Sedimentary rocks are formed when layers of sediment are cemented together due to pressure from layers above them. Metamorphic rocks are rocks which have been changed by heat, pressure and/or chemical action.

What to do

Provide the children with the collection of rocks. Encourage them to look for any similarities and differences between them. Allow them to use the hand lenses to study the rocks more closely and look, in particular, at things such as colour, shape, texture, size of grains, weight, smell, layering, sheen and so on. Ask them to find out how hard the rocks are by using a fingernail, coin and then the pointed end of a compass to scratch the surface. How easy is it to scratch?

Can they group the rocks in some way and provide reasons for their choice? Compare the criteria used with other groups of children.

Explain to the children what igneous, sedimentary and metamorphic rocks are and how they are formed. Tell them that they are going to group the rocks according to these three rock types by considering the size of the grains in the rocks.
• If large enough to be seen by the naked eye, they look interlocked and are all similar – metamorphic.
• If large enough to be seen with the naked eye, look glued together, and are made up of silt, sand or pebbles (may have fossils too) – sedimentary.
• If grains are not visible, rock is glassy or frothy – igneous.

Explain that this is only a rough guide and the children may need to use reference books to identify rocks accurately.

Follow-up

Conduct a survey of the rock types in your local area – to which of the three groups do they mainly belong? Find out about the uses of these rocks or the ores and minerals which are usually found with them.

Energy sources

Age range
Ten to eleven.

Group size
Whole class then groups of two to four.

What you need
Paper, pencils, reference books on energy sources, pictures of hydro-electric power stations, wind turbines, coal power stations and tidal barrages.

Science content
Fuels, waves and wind are all sources of energy. Most of the world's energy comes from fossil fuels such as coal, oil and gas. As these resources are beginning to run out, scientists are looking at alternative energy sources such as the sun, water and wind.

What to do
Ask the children to write down their definition of a fuel. Ask them to give some examples. Discuss their answers and talk about the uses of fuels such as coal, oil and gas. How are they used in homes/in power stations? What do they provide us with? Discuss what the children think energy means. Where can energy come from?

Explain to the children that most electricity in this country comes from power stations which use coal, oil or gas as their energy source. What are the advantages and disadvantages of using these sources of energy? Use the reference books or explain to the children how electricity is generated.

Discuss alternative methods of producing electricity such as wave and wind power. What are the advantages and disadvantages of using these sources of energy? Working in pairs or small groups, challenge the children to design and make a wind- or water-powered toy or machine.

Follow-up
Visit a power station, windmill or windfarm. Find out how the electricity is generated and how much is produced.

Burning fuels

Age range
Ten to eleven.

Group size
Two to four.

What you need
A candle, matches, a jar, modelling clay, a tablespoon, water.

Science content
Fuels can be burned to heat other things. Most fuels used today are fossil fuels – coal, oil and gas – but wood is another common fuel.

What to do

Discuss the term 'fuel' with the children. Can they give a definition of their own? What fuels can they name? Do they know how the fuels are used to provide us with electricity? Explain that they are going to do a simple experiment to see how fuels can be used to heat other things. This experiment will need close adult supervision because lighted candles are used.

Place a candle upright in a jar and secure the base with modelling clay so that the candle does not topple over. Light the candle. Explain to the children that the candle is the fuel which will be burned. Put a small amount of water in a tablespoon and hold this over the candle flame. Observe what happens. The water quickly begins to bubble and then boils.

Explain that this is what happens when fuels are burned in an electricity power station (Figure 1).

This is also similar to how a car engine works. The engine burns fuel in an enclosed chamber. As it burns, it releases gases which expand and move the pistons. The pistons are connected to a drive shaft which moves the wheels.

Discuss the fact that coal and wood can also be burned in households for heating purposes and that in some countries people still use wood fires for all their cooking and heating.

As a summary of the activity, ask the children to draw a flow diagram showing how a coal-fired power station generates electricity.

Follow-up

Consider heating, melting, boiling and the burning of materials. Which changes can be reversed? Which changes are not reversible? How could these changes be prevented?

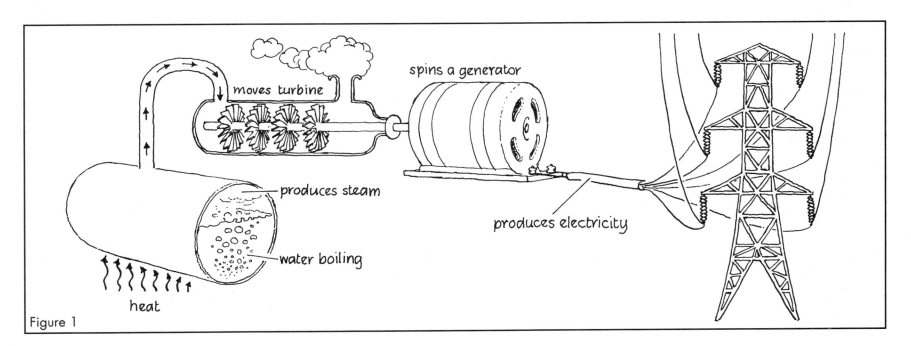

moves turbine
spins a generator
produces steam
produces electricity
water boiling
heat

Figure 1

DISPLAY IDEAS

• Make a collection of rocks and soils from the local area and a collection from a very different location. Display them on a table with hand lenses and question cards to encourage the children to look for similarities and differences between them. Mount photographs or posters showing the landforms in each area on the wall behind the collection.

• Make a sorting table for magnetic and non-magnetic things – provide objects, magnets and two small plastic rings for dividing these into sets.

• Make a display of building materials and pictures showing what these materials have been made from (such as timber beams – tree). Challenge the children to match the picture to the correct material.

• Display a collection of manufactured and natural materials. Provide two large hoops to encourage the children to sort the materials into two groups. Add pictures and posters of things the materials are used for. Write question cards which ask the children to match the material to the product.

• Mount pictures of fuels on a wall. Place a table below this and add the children's models of wind- or water-powered machines. Add diagrams showing how electricity can be produced from fuels as well as the children's diagrams of how their models work.

• Ask the children to write down descriptions of solids, liquids and gases. Add these to a collection of solids, liquids and gases. How well do the children's descriptions match each item? Also display the children's investigations of these materials.

• Design posters which 'advertise' a particular material such as wood or stone, showing its qualities and variety of uses. Make up radio advertisements and record these on tape. Display the tape with a collection of books about materials as well as a collection of the materials themselves.

• Challenge the children to design a house made entirely of one material such as wood or stone. Is it possible? Mount their results on the wall with writing describing the difficulties involved and how they could be overcome.

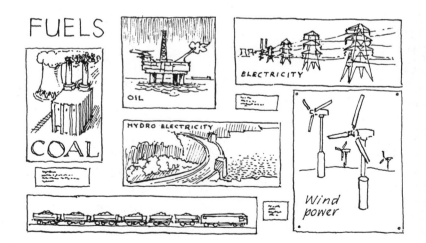

Links with other curriculum areas

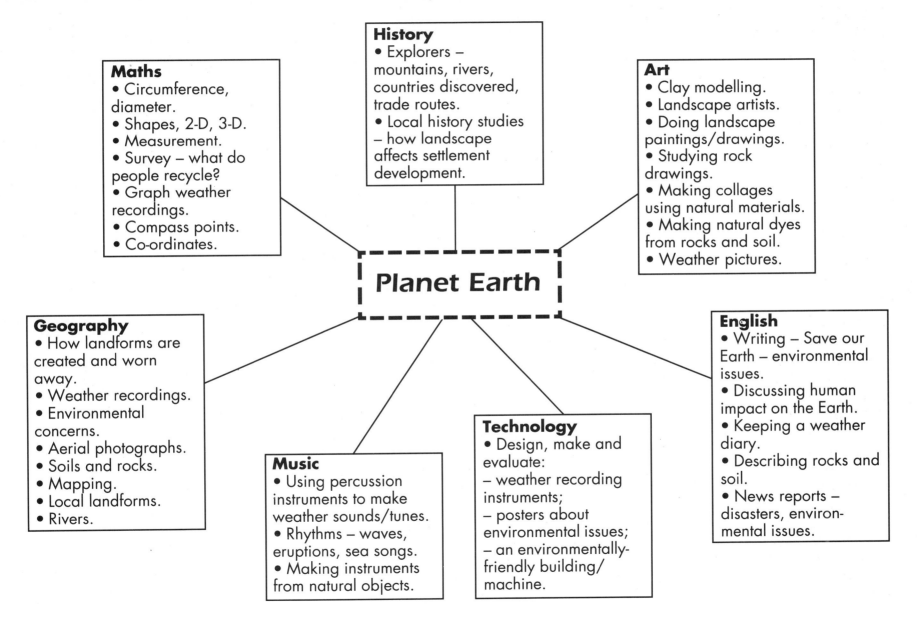

Maths
• Circumference, diameter.
• Shapes, 2-D, 3-D.
• Measurement.
• Survey – what do people recycle?
• Graph weather recordings.
• Compass points.
• Co-ordinates.

History
• Explorers – mountains, rivers, countries discovered, trade routes.
• Local history studies – how landscape affects settlement development.

Art
• Clay modelling.
• Landscape artists.
• Doing landscape paintings/drawings.
• Studying rock drawings.
• Making collages using natural materials.
• Making natural dyes from rocks and soil.
• Weather pictures.

Planet Earth

Geography
• How landforms are created and worn away.
• Weather recordings.
• Environmental concerns.
• Aerial photographs.
• Soils and rocks.
• Mapping.
• Local landforms.
• Rivers.

Music
• Using percussion instruments to make weather sounds/tunes.
• Rhythms – waves, eruptions, sea songs.
• Making instruments from natural objects.

Technology
• Design, make and evaluate:
– weather recording instruments;
– posters about environmental issues;
– an environmentally-friendly building/ machine.

English
• Writing – Save our Earth – environmental issues.
• Discussing human impact on the Earth.
• Keeping a weather diary.
• Describing rocks and soil.
• News reports – disasters, environmental issues.

Machines

This is a popular topic with children because it provides them with an opportunity to find out about how things work. It is very much a 'hands-on' topic in which the children can be encouraged to make their own models which move in some way. The topic links in very well with a history study of inventions as well as considering environmental aspects of energy use and transfer.

The children should be encouraged to investigate things such as the forces which make things move, how friction affects movement and how electricity can be used in machines. Such studies may inspire the children to design and make their own machines which actually work.

Pushes and pulls

Age range
Five to seven.

Group size
Two to four.

What you need
A collection of toys which work by pushing or pulling (or both) actions.

Science content
A push or pull is a force. The push or pull can make things work and can make things speed up or slow down.

What to do
Allow the children time to become familiar with the collection of toys. Let them play with them and ask them questions such as:
• Can you make the toy work?
• Which parts move?

• Can you say how it works?

Ask the children to sort the objects into two groups – those which you push to make work and those which you pull. The children may decide to make a third group of toys which use both actions. Discuss the findings with all the children. Do they all agree?

Can the children find other things in the classroom which they pull or push to work? Ask them to write or draw a list of these. Make a larger collection of things which you push and things which you pull. Cut out magazine pictures to add to this display.

Use the collection to make further investigations – for example, if you remove the wheels from a toy car what difference does this make to the ease of movement? Ask the children to look at the toy parts which make the pushes and pulls possible – for example wheels, string, levers. Can they find out exactly how the toy works?

Follow-up
Allow the children the opportunity to make their own toys which they work by pushing or pulling. This will lead into investigations of wheels, levers and possibly cogs.

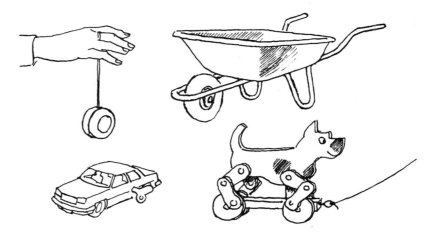

Wheels

Age range
Five to seven.

Group size
Two to four.

What you need
A collection of everyday objects such as: cardboard tubes, a tennis ball, a plastic jar, a pencil, a candle, an empty foil box, a die, a cotton reel, plastic lids, chalk, coins, boxes; dowelling or cane, modelling clay, round plastic lids of the same size, a craft knife.

Science content
Round objects roll more easily than objects which are not round. Rolling is affected by the object's weight, texture, shape and the surface on which it rolls. Axles must be level to ensure that the wheels balance.

What to do
Provide the group with the collection of everyday objects and ask them to predict which ones they think will roll. Ask them to say which ones they think will roll best and to give their reasons why. Then ask them to roll the objects and observe what happens. Record the results. The objects could be listed in order from best roller to worst. Encourage the children to look at this list and work out what makes the objects roll. Try rolling them on different surfaces, do you get the same results? What effect does the surface have on the ability of an object to roll? Which surface is best? Why? Which is worst?

Ask the children to name objects which use wheels. Make a list of these. Look at pictures of objects with wheels – look at the differences and similarities between them. Now explain to the children that they are going to make their own set of wheels using round plastic lids (see Figure 1).

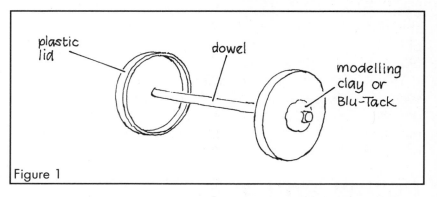

Figure 1

Make the holes in the lids for the children with a craft knife. Try to make the holes in the same place so that the axles line up straight. Let the children try out these wheels. Do they roll better than the other objects? Do they roll easily on different surfaces? Try slopes – do the wheels move faster? Why? Use different materials for the wheels such as stiff card, tin lids and so on. Which ones work best? Why?

Make a collection of objects which have wheels and put these on display with the wheels the children have made themselves.

Follow-up
Make a simple buggy using ice-cream containers or boxes and the same method of making wheels as above. Ensure that the holes for the axles are at the right height so the wheels touch the ground. Have a buggy race.

Levers

Age range
Six to eight.

Group size
Individuals or pairs.

What you need
A claw hammer, pliers, screwdriver, nutcracker, ruler, matchbox, bottle opener, a piece of wood with a nail hammered into it so that half of the nail is still showing, an empty treacle or paint tin with its lid firmly on, walnuts, a bottle from which the top has not been removed, a book, photocopiable page 126.

Science content
A lever is a simple machine used to make work easier. The pivot or fulcrum is the point where the lever turns. The load is placed at one end and effort is applied to the other end or pushing point. Levers work best when the pivot is close to the object and the pushing point is as far away as possible.

What to do
Place the wood with the nail hammered into it, the bottle, tin, walnut, matchbox and book on a table and ask the children to use the tools (pliers, screwdriver, nutcracker, ruler, bottle opener and hammer) to:
• open the bottle;
• lift the book up without using only their hands;
• open the tin;
• crack open the walnut;
• remove the nail from the wood.
   Ask them to find out which tool works best for each purpose and why. Discuss the notion of levers with the children – how they work and why we use them. Ask the children to find other examples of levers in the classroom. Then, using photocopiable page 126, ask the children to cut out the squares and sort the pictures into levers and non-levers. They can then stick the lever pictures to a piece of paper and add their own pictures, or worded list, of other levers found in their classroom/home.

Follow-up
Make a see-saw by balancing a ruler on a pencil with flat sides. Using two 2p coins, ask the children to place the coins on the ruler so that it balances. Then add another 2p coin to one end. Ask them to make it balance without adding another coin to the other side. What does this tell them about levers and the position of the load in relation to the pivot? (*Safety:* Close supervision is needed when using tools.)

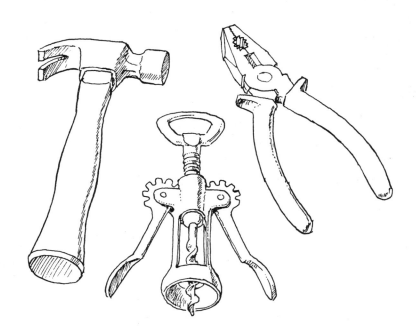

Friction

Age range
Seven to nine.

Group size
Two to four.

What you need
A toy car, four lengths of wood about 60cm long (one sanded smooth, one with lines of adhesive across it to make ridges about 10cm apart, one covered in a textured cloth and one covered in corrugated card), a measuring tape, a stopwatch.

Science content
When two objects rub together friction acts upon them. If the surface of the objects is rough or uneven, movement is more difficult. Friction thus affects the speed of an object. Speed can be calculated as distance travelled divided by the time taken.

What to do
The lengths of wood can be rested against a chair or table to make a ramp. Ask the children to measure how far the car travels along the floor after it has been rolled down each ramp. The children will need to think about how to make each test fair – the angle of the ramp, the amount of 'push' each time and how many turns on each ramp. (If you wish them to calculate speed also, one child will need to time how long each car takes from when it is pushed to when it reaches a given distance marked on the floor.) Ask them to record their findings in some way. On which surface does the car move most quickly? Can the children suggest why? Does the floor surface also make a

difference? The children could try out the ramps on other floor surfaces such as carpet, the playground and the hall to find out.

Follow-up
The angle of the ramp could be altered and the experiments repeated. Is there an optimum angle at which the car moves best? Investigate speed further. How difficult is it to stop the cars? Ask the children to place a building block at a set distance not far from the end of the ramp. Does this always stop the car? Relate this to road safety.

Cogs and gears

Age range
Seven to nine.

Group size
Two to four.

What you need
Round lids of different sizes, corrugated cardboard, nails, a hammer, a piece of wood, adhesive, a marker pen, pictures of cogs, cogs from bicycles.

Science content
Cogs play an important part in many machines. They make different parts of the machine move at different speeds or in different directions. If a small cog is engaged with a large cog, the smaller one will turn more times than the larger one and they will turn in different directions from each other.

What to do
Cut strips of corrugated cardboard wide enough to fit the edge of the lids. Stick these around the edges with the corrugated side facing outwards.

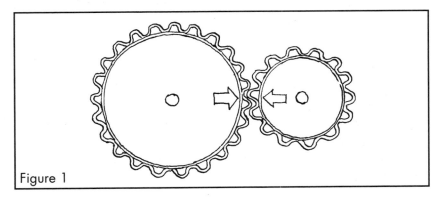

Figure 1

Nail one of your cogs to the piece of wood and then place a smaller cog next to it so that the 'teeth' of each cog meet. Nail this to the wood also so that the lids will turn freely. Use a marker pen to mark the lids at a place where the teeth meet, as shown in Figure 1.

Ask the children to turn the cogs and watch what happens. Do both cogs move the same way? How many times does the little cog turn when the big one has turned once? (Use the mark as a starting point and turn the big wheel once, counting the number of turns the little cog takes.) Then nail another cog of a different size to the wood (touching one of the other cogs) and observe what happens. Make a note of the direction in which each one turns and how many times they turn compared to the big cog. Which cog works the hardest?

Show the children pictures of cogs and old bicycle parts to discuss the uses of cogs and how they work on simple machines such as an egg-whisk.

Follow-up
Make a simple toy or model using the cogs the children have made. Cut out pictures of animals and stick these to the large cog to make a fairground roundabout. Encourage the children to think of other toys they could make with the cogs.

Making a circuit

Age range
Eight to eleven.

Group size
Individuals or pairs.

What you need
A 1.5v battery and 1.5v bulb, pieces of insulated wire with bare ends, a bulb holder, small screwdriver, sticking tape.

Science content
A complete circuit is needed before the bulb will light up (see Figure 1). Electricity is a flow of electrons. Ampère, a scientist, made an incorrect guess when he was investigating the flow of electricity. He maintained that the flow went from positive to negative and this statement has been absorbed into literature and practice and is still recognised all over the world. More recently, however, scientists have discovered that this is incorrect and that electricity actually flows from negative to positive. It flows in one direction only (this can be proved by trying out a buzzer which will only work if the wires are placed on the correct ends of the battery). The bulb lights up because the filament is made of very thin, coiled wire made of a different metal. The electricity meets greater resistance when it meets the filament and 'works harder', causing the thin wire to heat up, giving off light. An inert gas in the bulb prevents it bursting into flames.

What to do
Supply the children with the equipment they need and let them try out their own ideas of how to get the bulb to light up. If they become frustrated, prompt them by using such questions as:

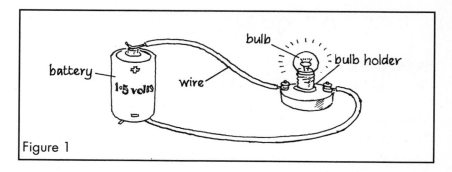
Figure 1

- Why are there two wires?
- Where do you think they go?
- How many ends are there on the battery?
- Do we need to touch both ends with the wires?
- How do you think the wires join to the bulb holder?
- Why are there screws on the bulb holder?
- Where does the bulb go?

Once they have managed to light the bulb, ask them the following questions (depending on age and experience):
- Where does the electricity come from?
- In which direction is the electricity flowing?
- If we remove one wire why does the bulb not light up?
- Which part of the bulb lights up?
- Why does the bulb light up?

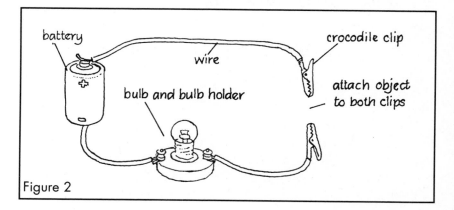
Figure 2

Ask the children to draw their circuit and mark on it with arrows the direction of the flow of electricity.

Follow-up

Ask the children to test out which materials will allow electricity to pass through them (conductors). Collect various objects made from metal, wood, paper and plastic and test them using a circuit like the one shown in Figure 2. Place the objects between the crocodile clips one at a time. Does the bulb light up? Record the results.

Using switches

Age range

Nine to eleven.

Group size

Individual or pairs.

What you need

Two 1.5v batteries, a 3v bulb, a bulb holder, a small screwdriver, three pieces of insulated wire with the ends bare, paper-clips, paper-fasteners, a cardboard tube, foil, card, scissors, adhesive, sticking tape.

Science content

A switch is used to turn electricity on and off. When the switch is off, the circuit is not complete so the electricity cannot flow to all parts of the circuit.

What to do

Provide the children with a piece of card, two paper-clips, two paper-fasteners, three pieces of wire, a battery and a bulb and holder then challenge them to make a switch which will turn the bulb on and off. If they have trouble in doing

this, show them how the paper-clips can be attached to the card (Figure 1) and then ask them to join up the circuit to the clips. If the bulb does not light, ask them for possible reasons why – the wires are not attached correctly, the bulb is not screwed in properly, the bulb has 'blown', the wires are not securely taped to the battery and so on. Encourage them to check each part of the circuit for possible faults.

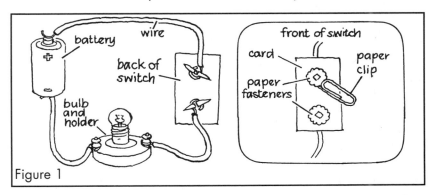

Figure 1

Then explain that they are going to make a torch. Provide a cardboard tube, some card to make a cone, metal foil to line the inside of the cone and another battery. Again, allow them to experiment but if they struggle, make useful suggestions based on Figure 2.

Follow-up

Experiment with buzzers as well as bulbs.

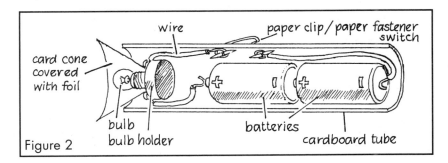

Figure 2

Series circuits

Age group
Nine to eleven

Group size
Two to four.

What you need
A 1.5v battery, at least two bulb holders, at least two small bulbs, at least four pieces of insulated wire with ends bare, a small screwdriver, adhesive tape.

Science content
If all the parts of an electrical circuit are joined in a single loop, the circuit is connected in a series. The second bulb in a series circuit will be less bright than the first bulb because the same amount of energy is shared between the two bulbs. If the flow of electricity is likened to a continuous series of coal trucks with coal (energy) inside them, then as the trucks move through the bulb, some of this energy will be used to light the bulb (the energy has been changed to heat and light energy). The second bulb will therefore have less energy to light it.

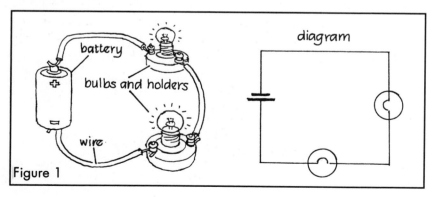
Figure 1

What to do
Ask the children to make a circuit using two bulbs so that the circuit is in one single loop (Figure 1). What do they notice about the brightness of the bulbs? If they unscrew one bulb, what happens? If two batteries are connected instead of one what happens? (Ensure that the bulbs can take the additional voltage.) How many bulbs can they join in a series and still make all the bulbs light up? Can they add a switch to the circuit? What are the disadvantages of a series circuit?

Ask the children to draw their circuit, using arrows to indicate the direction of the flow of electricity.

Follow-up
Provide the children with diagrams of series circuits and ask them to construct the circuit as it is shown in the diagram.

Motors

Age range
Nine to eleven.

Group size
Two to four.

What you need
A small motor, insulated wire with bare ends, a 1.5v battery, stiff cardboard, paper-clips, paper-fasteners, sticking tape, two bar magnets, string, an old motor (optional).

Science content
An electric motor changes electrical energy into mechancial energy. Inside a motor is a wheel called a rotor. Near the rotor is a coil of wire through which electricity flows. This

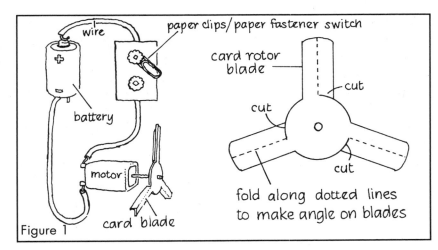

wire

paper clips/paper fastener switch

card rotor blade

cut

cut

cut

battery

motor

card blade

fold along dotted lines to make angle on blades

Figure 1

causes the wire to become a magnet. It magnetises the metal that surrounds the rotor and the magnetic forces in this metal pull on the rotor causing it to spin.

What to do

If possible, take apart an old motor to show the children what is inside it. Ask them to look at it closely and see if they can provide reasons for how the motor works. If they do not know, briefly explain it to them.

Then allow them to see how the spinning effect can be created with magnets by using two bar magnets. Hang one on a thread and hold the other so that one end of the magnet is near an end of the hanging magnet. The hanging magnet will begin to turn. Keep changing the ends of the hand-held magnet so that first one pole and then the other is facing the end of the hanging magnet, causing it to spin.

The children could then make a model fan (Figure 1) to help them understand more fully how a motor can move things.

Follow-up

Allow the children to make their own model 'machine' using a constructon kit, motor, pulley, battery and rubber band.

Logic gates

Age range

Ten to eleven.

Group size

Two to four.

What you need

A 1.5v battery, 6 pieces of insulated wire with bare ends, a bulb holder, bulb, small screwdriver, buzzer, two switches.

Science content

A gate can be used to let things in or keep things out. In electrical logic gates, switches can be used to open and close circuits, acting like gates. An AND gate has two inputs (switches) and its output will only be on if both of its inputs are on (the bulb will only light up if both switches are on). In an OR gate, either input can be on to make the output on (either switch can make the bulb light up).

What to do

Help the children to set up a circuit as shown in Figure 1 (overleaf). Ask them to explain why the bulb will only light up if the two switches are on. Try with only one switch on to see what happens. Challenge them to make another circuit using two switches that will work in a different way – that is, the bulb will light up if only one of the switches is on.

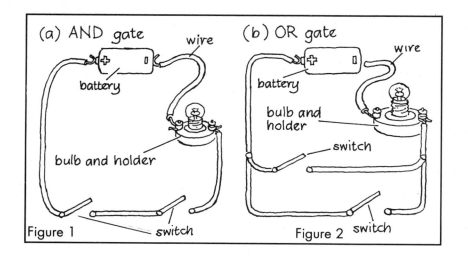

(a) AND gate

wire

battery

bulb and holder

Figure 1

switch

(b) OR gate

wire

battery

bulb and holder

switch

Figure 2

switch

If the children cannot work out the circuit themselves, help them to make a circuit like the one shown in Figure 2. Ask them to try to explain why the bulb will light if only one switch is on this time.

Can they develop this further and make a circuit in which a bulb and/or a buzzer can be made to turn on and off? How many bulbs and buzzers can they make to turn on and off or work together?

Follow-up

Make a model house where switches can be used to turn lights on and off and a burglar alarm (buzzer) which will only work if the door is opened but will work whether the lights are on or off.

DISPLAY IDEAS

• Take an old bicycle apart and display the pieces. Can the children work out which parts go where and why?

• Make a display of a collection of toys which move in some way. Put up some question cards which encourage the children to think about how the toys work.

• Use a table to display some everyday objects such as cans, cloth, egg cartons, play dough and so on. Make some question cards challenging the children to try different experiments with the objects such as changing the shape, rolling it down a slope, finding out whether it will conduct electricity and so on.

• Make model machines and display them alongside the children's investigations about gears, wheels and levers.

• Put up pictures of things which use electricity and display them with children's safety posters about using electricity.

• Make model houses or lighthouses with working lights. Display them with a flow chart showing how electricity is generated and how it gets to the house/ lighthouse.

• Make a display of a collection of wheels including wheels the children have made and their writing about wheels and ramp investigations. Add road safety posters.

• Put up pictures of machines and display questions about them asking which ones have motors/wheels/ levers/pulleys and so on? Add the results from a survey about the number and type of machines found in the home or school.

• Make two/three huge cogs with handles and mount them on the wall so that they can be turned. Display the children's writing about cog investigations.

• Set up a shop in the classroom which sells electrical parts so that the children become familiar with the names of the items.

Links with other curriculum areas

Technology
• Designing, making and evaluating:
– an invented machine or robot;
– a logo for the machine;
– a company name;
– an advertising poster;
– a toy or puppet using levers, cogs, rubber bands.

Maths
• Conduct a survey of machines used at home.
• Conduct a survey among the children – what machine would they like to be invented? Graph the survey results.
• Make function machines.
• Draw plans of machines and shapes in machines.

Art
• Pencil drawings of machines.
• Rubbings of machine parts, e.g. cogs.
• Making collages.
• Making 3-D models.

Music
• Making machine sounds.
• Making TV jingles to advertise machines.
• Imitating the rhythms of machines.

Machines

English
• Listening to/reading stories about machines.
• Writing stories/poems.
• Writing an instruction booklet about your own invention.
• Writing advertisements to sell machines.
• Inventing crosswords, word searches.
• Drama – machine movements, sounds.

History
• The development of machinery in relation to farming, transport, printing, domestic life.
• Early machines – for example Egyptian Shadoof, plough, wheel.
• Tracing the development of one machine, for example the car.
• How have machines helped people?

Geography
• Look at:
– resources used by machines and used to make machines. Map countries;
– reasons for settlement – Industrial Revolution;
– local area industries; road and rail links.

Structures

Everywhere you look there are structures of one kind or another and each of these structures is made up of materials. This topic thus provides a good basis for the study of materials, both natural and manufactured, as well as the strength, flexibility and forces which play a part in the design of structures.

Through investigative work the children can begin to understand how materials can be joined or bonded together, what the strongest shape is for certain structures, what material is best for constructing specific things and to appreciate how important structures are for humans today.

Building materials

Age range
Five to seven.

Group size
Four to six.

What you need
Samples of building materials such as different types of bricks, tiles, wood, pipes, sand, cement, gravel; pictures or photographs of buildings at different stages of construction.

Science content
Different materials have different properties of strength, flexibility and use. There will be differences and similarities in terms of their texture, shape, colour and hardness. Certain materials are more suited for a particular purpose than other materials.

What to do
Talk to the children about how houses are built. Use pictures or photographs to show the various stages of construction. If possible, visit a local building site (safety precautions are very important here). Ask the children why certain things are done, for example the foundations, why walls are usually brick, and so on. Their answers will indicate their level of understanding about the materials used in buildings and will point the direction in which to make further investigations.

Provide each group with a collection of building materials. Ask them to tell you where they think each one would be used in building a house. Ask them about their own homes – what materials are there in their houses? Can they see any of these materials in their classroom/school?

Allow the children to look at and touch the materials. Let them describe the materials to you – colour, shape, smell, texture and so on. Can they find differences and similarities between the samples?

Next, ask the children to sort the materials into groups and give reasons for their choices. Can other children guess how the materials have been grouped. They could draw their groups and compare their groupings with others.

Follow-up
Make cards with words or pictures on so that the children can match the materials to the cards according to shape, colour, use, size, texture and so on. Cut out pictures of parts of buildings showing the materials – can the children match the picture to the material?

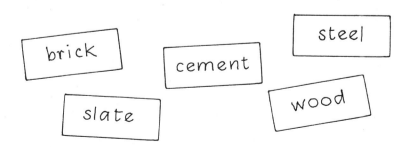

Changing shapes

Age range
Five to seven.

Group size
Four to six.

What you need
An aluminium drink can, modelling clay, a plastic drinking straw, balloon, elastic band, paper, copper wire, pipe-cleaner, old pair of tights, cloth, wood, nail.

Science content
Some objects can change shape by stretching, twisting, bending, pulling and pushing. If an object reverts back to its original shape it has elasticity. Rigidity refers to how strongly the object resists changing its shape.

What to do
Provide the children with the collection of objects and ask them to predict which ones they think they could change the shape of in some way. Ask them to group or draw these objects as a record of their predictions.

Then ask them to test out the materials. Can they change the shape by stretching/twisting/bending/pulling/pushing?

Can some objects be changed in more than one way? Which shapes are the easiest to change? Why? Do the 'easy-to-change' objects have something in common? Do the hard-to-change objects have something in common? Why do some objects need to change shape and others not? How could some objects be made more rigid? Encourage the children to record their findings in some way by drawing groups of things which stretch, twist, bend and so on.

Follow-up
Use the collection of objects for further investigations – for example take all the objects which stretch and find a way of testing which one stretches the most. Can they find out which one is the strongest?

Using the right material

Age range
Six to eight.

Group size
Two to four.

What you need
A length of wood, thick card, thin card, corrugated card, paper, cloth, metal foil, tissue-paper, about eight heavy books, a toy car.

Science content
It is not only the shape of a structure which is important, but the materials of which the structure is made. The materials chosen will depend on the job the structure is used for. Some structures need to be rigid and others flexible. Aesthetics is also often considered – what will the structure

look like if it is made from a particular material? The cost of the material may also need consideration as well as its availability.

What to do
Provide the group with all the materials and ask them to consider which one they think would make a good span (beam) for a bridge. Consider each material individually and ask the children to look at it closely. How strong is it? Does it bend? Does it stretch? Would it sag? Ask the children to predict which one would make the best beam and perhaps rank the others in order as well.

Then ask them to test all the materials by placing them between two piles of books. Use a toy car to see if the bridge will hold any weight. Ask the children to draw or write about what happens. Were their predictions correct? What are the properties of the best material? Could a real bridge be made from this? Why/why not?

Challenge the children to try to make the bendy materials more rigid – can they be folded or shaped in some way that will make a stronger beam? Record the results.

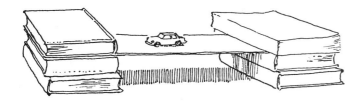

Follow-up
Using one, or all, of the materials used in this activity, challenge the children to find as many uses as they can for the material. Look around the classroom. How many uses are there for wood, for example?

Walls

Age range
Six to seven.

Group size
Individuals or pairs.

What you need
Rectangular wooden blocks or building blocks, cardboard tubes, thin card, newspaper, thick card, a soft sponge ball, adhesive tape.

Science content
When building a wall, materials are usually chosen for the particular properties that make them suitable for the purpose. Materials used to build are usually strong and can be bonded easily. Walls can be made stronger if the bricks are interlocked and careful interlocking can even eliminate the need for a bonding material, as is evident in dry stone walls. The higher the wall, the more stability required, therefore a good base is needed.

What to do
Ask the children to make a wall that will stand up using newspaper. How can they make sure it stays upright? Is the newspaper itself too flexible? Do they think it is a suitable material for a wall?

Ask them to make walls from the other materials (card, tubes, building blocks). Which material do they think makes the best wall? Why? What properties do walls need to make them strong? Is the base of the wall important? Why?

Ask them to make a wall using the building blocks as shown in Figure 1 (overleaf). Then ask them to gently roll the sponge ball against the wall. What happens? Does the

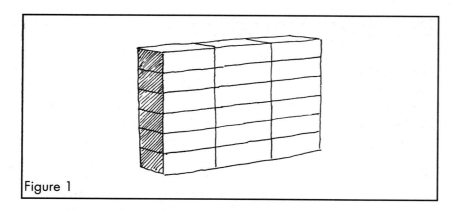

Figure 1

wall collapse? If not, throw the ball slightly harder – what happens?

Next, make a wall like the one shown in Figure 2. Roll the ball against the wall as before and note what happens. Is this wall stronger than the first? Why?

Allow them to experiment with making walls of different heights. How high can they build a wall from each of the materials without it falling over? What makes high walls strong and stable?

Figure 2

Follow-up
Look at walls in the local area. What are they made of? What has been used to cement them together? Have any walls collapsed? What do you think has caused this?

Making strong shapes

Age range
Seven to nine.

Group size
Individuals or pairs.

What you need
A4 thin card or paper, measuring weights, four building blocks of the same size, adhesive tape.

Science content
The shape of a structure greatly influences the strength and flexibility of that structure. This means that a single material can have a variety of uses depending on the shape it is formed into.

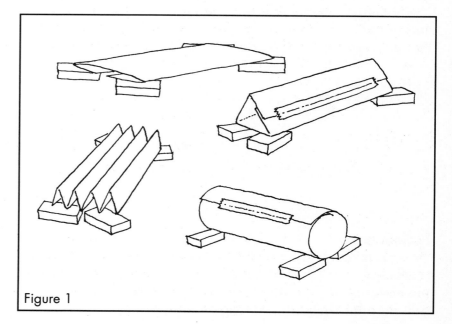

Figure 1

What to do

Challenge the children to make different shaped bridges from the card. Which will hold the most weight when supported by the four blocks? Ask them to record all the designs they tried and how much weight they each held before collapsing. Some ideas they might try are represented in Figure 1.

Can the children suggest why some shapes are stronger than others? Which shapes are more commonly used in real bridges? Can some of these shapes hold our own weight? Try it! Does the ability of a material to change shape influence what it is used for? Can the children think of examples?

Follow-up

Challenge the children to make the tallest, free-standing tower they can using five sheets of newspaper and a metre of sticking tape. They can put the knowledge gained from the bridge investigation to good use as they will be more aware of the strength of particular shapes.

Bonding materials

Age range
Eight to ten.

Group size
Two to four.

What you need
Adhesive tape, masking tape, insulation tape, a selection of different adhesives, paper-clips, a stapler, paper-fasteners, A4 paper (enough sheets to test each joining material), scissors, measuring weights.

Science content
The way a structure is joined together affects its strength and rigidity. Certain adhesives are more suitable for bonding particular materials than others. A comparison can be made between adhesives on the basis of their strength and flexibility. An understanding of this will help children to select the correct adhesives for everyday uses.

What to do
Ask the children to cut the piece of paper in half (lengthways). Then ask them to look at each type of bonding material to predict which ones they think will be best for joining the two pieces of paper so that a strong join is made. They will need to read the labels on the adhesives carefully so that they find out what they can be used for and how to use them correctly. Ask them to write down their predictions before they begin the investigation.

Then ask them to test each bonding material to see if their predictions were correct. They will need to consider how to make the investigation a fair test. Which factor is being changed each time? Which factors stay the same? How will

the result be measured? Consideration will thus need to be given to the following:
• How much adhesive/tape is applied each time.
• How long they wait before testing it and how they will test the strength.
• Is the strongest the one which holds the most weight or the one which resists most when you try to pull the pieces apart? If the paper tears but the join holds, how will this affect the test?

Ask the children to record their results in some way. Can they say what makes some bonding materials stronger than others? Were their predictions correct? How will the results affect other tasks they do at school? Will it help them to choose the best bonding material for their needs?

Follow-up

• Try the same test using things other than paper – such as metal foil, cloth, balsa wood. Do you get the same results?
• Find out what particular adhesives are made from.
• Try making adhesive paste from flour and water – how strong is this?

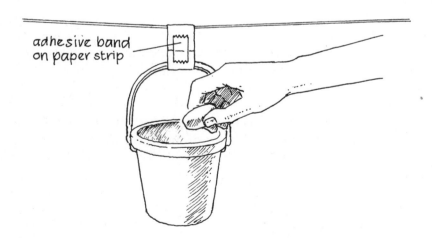

adhesive band on paper strip

Insulating buildings

Age range
Eight to ten.

Group size
Two to four.

What you need
Eight empty drink cans (all the same size), thermometers, warm water, a measuring jug, modelling clay, a stopwatch, graph paper, cotton wool, thick fabric, a piece of carpet, newspaper, metal foil, plastic bubble wrap, foam, rubber bands, a pencil, paper.

Science content
Buildings are insulated to prevent heat loss from walls, floors, windows and roofs. Some materials are better thermal insulators than others. Common insulators used in buildings are carpets, loft insulation, wall cavity insulation and double glazing.

What to do
Talk to the children about insulation used in buildings. Do they know what an insulator is? What materials are used to insulate their homes? Which parts of their homes are insulated? Why is this?

Explain that they are going to test some materials to find out which one is the best insulator. Show them the selection of materials and allow them time to look closely at each one to observe the similarities and differences between them. Ask them to predict which materials would be good insulators and why.

Cover seven cans each with a different material. Secure the material in place with rubber bands. Keep the eighth can uncovered to use as a control. The cans can be tested with the control can one at a time or all at once. Pour an equal amount of warm water into all of the cans and measure the temperature. Ensure the temperature is the same in each can at the beginning of the experiment. Once the temperature has been measured and recorded, cover the hole in the cans with modelling clay to prevent further heat loss.

Measure and record the temperature of the water inside each can at regular intervals, say every 30 seconds or one minute. Leave the thermometer inside the can for a few seconds to ensure a steady reading. Reseal the hole in the can each time after taking the temperature.

Draw a graph to show the changes in temperature for each can. Which material kept the water the warmest for longest? Why is this material a good insulator? Is this material used in buildings for insulation. Where? Which material was the poorest insulator? Can the children suggest why?

Follow-up

Loose materials such as sand, feathers, polystyrene balls, straw, wood chips and soil could be tested in the same way by placing the cans in a box and filling the box with the material. Which material is the best insulator? Why?

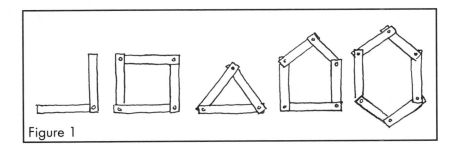

Figure 1

Building frames

Age range
Eight to ten.

Group size
Two to four.

What you need
Strips of thick card (approximately 10cm long and 1cm wide), paper-fasteners (or construction kit lengths and fasteners), pictures of building frames and structures such as roof rafters.

Science content
A frame provides strength and structure to a building. The triangle is a very stable shape. When a force is exerted on a triangular shape, all the sides work together to hold it in place. Triangular girders are used in buildings and bridges to provide stability. The triangular shape of roof rafters is stable because the rafters push against each other with equal and opposite forces.

What to do
Ask the children to join the strips of card together to make different shaped frames (Figure 1).

Ask them to push gently on to the sides of each shape. What happens? Can the shape of the triangle be changed by pushing at a corner? What do you need to do to the triangle to change its shape? Which of the five shapes is the strongest? Can the children say why? Can a weak shape be made stronger by adding more pieces of card?

Relate what has been discovered to building frames. Look at pictures or visit a building site (safety considerations will be necessary here). What shapes are used? Are triangular shapes common as braces? Identify the balanced forces in the structure of the building.

Follow-up

Make three-dimensional shapes such as a cube and pyramid. Push the corners and observe what happens. Which shape offers more resistance to movement? Why? Discuss the forces involved. Are they balanced?

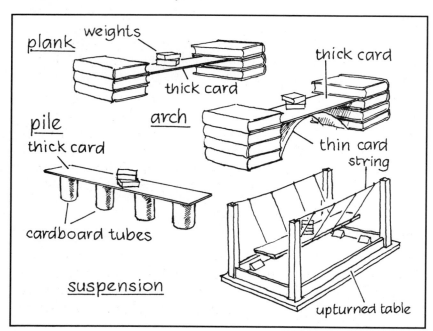

Bridges

Age range
Nine to eleven.

Group size
Two to four.

What you need
Cardboard tubes, thin and thick card, scissors, adhesive, adhesive tape, string, measuring weights, about eight heavy books.

Science content
Bridge beams can be supported by arches, piles or the use of suspended cables. These give the bridge stability and strength. The shape of a bridge is designed to distribute the load evenly to reduce stress. Thus the force of a load does not act in one place only, there are many smaller forces acting across the whole bridge. The forces are equal and balanced which ensures that there is no movement in the structure. Forces can be represented on a diagram by the use of arrows.

What to do
Ask the children to make the bridges shown in the illustration on the left. Can they predict which bridge will be the strongest? Let them use measuring weights to test out which bridge holds the most weight before it collapses. Can the children suggest why the strongest bridge is stronger than the others? How important are the bridge supports? What other shape works well as a support? Try using triangles and rectangles.

Ask the children to draw diagrams of their bridges. Can they draw arrows on the diagrams to show where forces are acting? Compare their answers with others and discuss the results. Do they all agree? If the forces were unbalanced, what would happen to the bridge?

Follow-up
Find out about the keystone on arch bridges. Visit bridges to look at how they are constructed. What materials are used? What shapes are used?

Sources of building materials

Age range
Nine to eleven.

Group size
Individuals or pairs.

What you need
Photocopiable page 127, a pencil, reference books on materials – what they are made from, how they are made and so on.

Science content
Buildings use materials which come from a range of sources. Some of these materials are used in their natural state (such as wood), whereas others have been manufactured by humans (such as steel and plastic).

What to do
Discuss the photocopiable sheet with the children. Explain how to fill it in correctly. Help the children to decide what things are made from by using the classroom as an example before completing the sheet. What are the classroom doors made from? Do you know what glass is made from?

 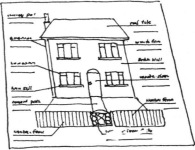

Help the children to use the reference books to find out the answers to things they do not know already. (Answers: chimney pot – clay, PVC guttering and drainpipe – oil, glass window – sand, stone lintel – sandstone, stainless steel doorknob - iron ore, roof tile - clay, brick wall – clay, aluminium window frame – bauxite, wooden door – trees, cement path – lime and clay, wrought-iron gate – iron ore, wooden fence – trees.)

Discuss their results. Talk about the fact that other materials can be used for each of these house parts and help the children to draw up a list of alternative materials. Discuss these alternatives. Which ones are best and why? For example, are wooden, aluminium or plastic window frames best? Are most materials used to build the house manufactured? Where do these materials come from originally? How are they made? Find out what the frames and foundations of houses are made from. Do all countries use these materials? Why/why not?

Follow-up
Find out what things are made from in the children's own homes – consider cloths such as curtains and furniture coverings, types of wood in furniture, carpet fabrics and so on. What are the most common sources of these materials? How are they made?

DISPLAY IDEAS

• Take photographs of bridges and/or buildings in your area and use for a wall display. Add a table with three-dimensional models of buildings/bridges.

• Build a house in the corner of the classroom. Display writing about wall, foundation or frame investigations on its walls.

• Take photographs of building parts. Mount these on the wall and attach string to name labels showing the material from which each object is made. Add a map showing where in the world these materials come from.

• Wall mount paper which has been made into different shapes. Add writing about a 'making paper stronger' investigation.

• Make bridges, stools or houses from paper and card and hang these from string like a mobile so that all sides of the structure can be seen.

• Make a display of building materials – include hand lenses to encourage children to take a closer look.

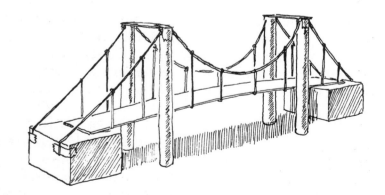

• Cut out magazine pictures of very tall buildings and towers and mount these on the wall. Add a table of the children's own towers and tall structures.

• Make a book of children's drawings and/or photographs of structures in the local area. Add information to show where they are, how old they are, what materials they are made of, what they are used for and so on.

• Find out about the world's tallest/widest or best known structures. Make scale models or silhouettes of them and display these alongside a scale model or silhouette of the school building.

• Make a display using photographs of the children's own homes. Write captions which encourage the children to consider things such as shapes, building materials used, size, similarities and differences and so on.

• Find out about famous world bridges. Mount the information on a wall display together with the children's own model bridges.

• Make three-dimensional shapes then stick them to card and mount on the wall so that the shapes stick out.

Links with other curriculum areas

English
- Writing about 'my house'.
- Stories about houses, buildings, bridges.
- Story writing – haunted house, trapped in a tunnel and so on.
- Discussion – is the Channel Tunnel a good idea?
- Writing poems about buildings, bridges, tunnels.

RE
- Studying religious buildings, tombs, burial mounds.
- Christian stories such as 'The Fall of Jericho'.

Music
- Listening to/singing songs about building bridges.
- Making sounds to do with building a house.

Technology
- Designing, making and evaluating bridges, towers or houses.
- Which material is best to make a model tower?
- Making posters about home safety, dangers of building sites and so on.
- Using construction kits to make structures.
- Designing a dream home.

Structures

History
- Roman, Anglo-Saxon or Viking buildings, structures, road building.
- The architecture of Tudor, Victorian and more recent times.
- Railway construction in Victorian times.
- How buildings change over time.
- Structures in ancient times – Greece, Egypt.
- The history of bridges.
- The Berlin Wall.

Maths
- Drawing rooms/ buildings to scale.
- Using plans.
- Measuring rooms, buildings, school.
- Estimating the length of structures.
- Weight – how much my bridge will hold.
- Shapes — 2-D and 3-D shapes in structures.
- Counting – spans, doors, windows and so on.

Art
- Making:
  - rubbings of building surfaces;
  - paintings of local houses, bridges;
  - collages of local buildings;
  - clay models of structures.
- Stained glass windows of churches.
- Looking at artists who have painted buildings.

Geography
- Maps, plans of buildings. Use of scale. Measurement.
- Locating famous structures round the world on a map – Pyramids, Eiffel Tower.
- Comparing buildings in different countries – materials used, uses of.
- Finding out where building materials come from – locate on map.
- Comparing buildings/ structures in the local area with another place.
- Environmental issues involved in using materials for building.

Space

Children of all ages are fascinated by this topic. They are keen to learn about space travel and what life might be like on other planets. Another interesting aspect is investigating the Earth's own part in the solar system and how day and night and length of year occur.

This leads on to the study of light. Children can learn about sources of light, how light travels, how shadows are formed, how light can be reflected and how our eyes see things.

The topic thus provides many opportunities for firsthand investigations as well as studies of a more instructional nature.

Sources of light

Age range
Five to seven.

Group size
Small groups or whole class.

What you need
A variety of torches, candles, reflective objects, matches, a room which can be darkened.

Science content
Darkness is the absence of light. Light can come from natural sources – the sun and the cycle of day and night, lightning – and artificial sources – torches, candles and so on.

What to do
Prepare a room so that it is dark before you take the children there. Place the torches, candles, reflective objects and matches in a box and take this with you into the room.

Explain to the children that they are going into a dark room so that they are prepared for it. Once inside, sit them down in a circle. Ask them what they can see around them in the darkness. Then, as their eyes get used to the dark, ask them again – they will gradually be able to see more things. Ask them to tell you why it is dark in the room. Why is it dark at night time? How could we make the room light now?

Next, take a torch out of the box and turn it on. Ask the children to tell you what is making the light. Shine the torch around the room and ask the children to tell you what they notice about the light (straight line, size of beam, how far it reaches and so on).

Turn on different-sized torches and compare the size and length of their beams. Ask a child to hold a reflective object at various places round the room, notice how well the torch picks up the object. Discuss the importance of reflective strips on clothing for road safety purposes.

Light a candle and compare the strength of candlelight with the torches. Is the beam different? Why? What causes the light to flicker? How many candles will need to be lit to equal the strongest torch? Test this out. (Adult supervision is important here.)

Then open the curtains in the room one at a time and ask the children to tell you about the light. Is it stronger than the torch and candles? Why? Is the light a different colour? Does it illuminate a larger area? Where is this light coming from? Gradually open the curtains so that the whole room is light. What things can the children now see that they couldn't before? Do the reflective objects show up as much now? Why not? Turn on the torch and light the candle – does the light look as bright as before? Why not?

Ask the children to draw as many things as they can think of which give out light – torches, lamps, TV, sun. Display their drawings alongside various torches and lamps.

Follow-up
• Observe candle flames more closely – note the colours of the flame and what happens to the wick and the wax.
• The children can make their own light using a battery, bulb and wires.

Movement of the sun

Age range
Six to seven.

Group size
Small groups or whole class.

What you need
A sunny day, a paper and pencil, a stick or free-standing post, stones or markers.

Science content
The sun appears to move across the sky as the day progresses. What is actually happening is that the Earth is rotating on its axis. One complete rotation takes 24 hours. The sun looks low in the morning, high in the middle of the day and low in the evening. The shortest shadows are found at midday when the sun is at its highest.

What to do
Choose a sunny day and ask the children to draw the position of the sun at various times throughout the day – by looking in the playground or through a window. (*Safety:* Make sure the children do not look directly at the sun as permanent eye damage can be caused.) Discuss the drawings with the children. What does the sun appear to do? At what part of the day was the sun highest in the sky? At what time was it lowest?

Explain that it is not the sun which is moving but the Earth spinning round. Demonstrate this by asking the children to stand up and turn slowly from west to east. The surroundings will appear to move from east to west. This is the same as the Earth's rotation – it spins from west to east, making the sky appear to move from east to west.

Choose another sunny day and place a stick in the ground to mark the movement of shadows throughout the day. Can the children tell the time using the shadow stick? When was the shortest shadow? Why? When was the longest shadow? Why?

Follow-up

Keep a record of the lengths of shadows from the shadow stick throughout the year. In which season are the shadows longest? Why? When are they shorter? Why?

Seasons

Age range
Six to seven.

Group size
Small groups or whole class.

What you need
Pictures showing the four seasons, paper, pencils.

Science content
The Earth rotates around a tilted axis so the north and south poles lean towards the sun at different times of the year. The winter and summer solstice refers to the two times of the year when the sun is furthest from the Equator. In the northern hemisphere, the summer solstice (when the sun is furthest north from the Equator) is around June 21. This marks the beginning of summer and is the day with the most hours of daylight. The winter solstice is around December 22 which marks the beginning of winter and the day with the least hours of daylight. The seasons are reversed in the southern hemisphere.

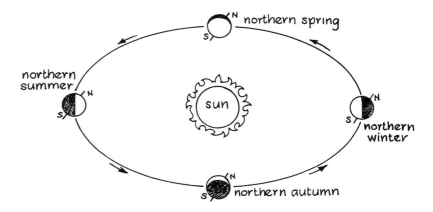

What to do

Ask the children to look at the pictures showing the seasons. Can they tell which season the pictures represent? What clues tell them this? Write a list of the things the children associated with each season in each picture. Ask the children to tell you what happens to trees and animals during different seasons. What kinds of flowers do we find in different seasons?

Go outside and look for clues that tell the children what season it is. Do they know which season will come next? What might happen to the trees, plants and animals you find outside during the next season?

Ask the children to draw a picture of each season. Ask them to include a tree and the kinds of animals and plants they may find. If humans are in the picture, discuss the types of clothing which might be worn and why.

Follow-up

Make a display of the clothing types which may be worn in each season. Carry out investigations using the material from which the clothes are made. For example, test for waterproofing by using an eye dropper of water and placing it on each material. Does the water come through? Which material would be best for a raincoat?

Shadows

Age range

Eight to nine.

Group size

Two to four.

What you need

A torch, a clear glass bottle or other transparent object, tracing paper or other translucent object, a book or other opaque object.

Science content

Light can travel through some things and not others. If the light does not pass through the object, shadows are formed. Transparent objects allow light to pass through them, translucent objects let light through but it is diffused or scattered and opaque objects do not let any light pass through them.

What to do

Invite the children to look closely at the collection of objects and ask them to predict which ones they think the torch light will shine through. Can they give reasons for their choices?

Let them test this out by shining a torch through the objects on to a wall. Discuss the differences observed between the transparent and the translucent objects. How different does the light on the wall look? What do the children think is happening to cause this?

Encourage the children to use other objects to see if the light will shine through. What do all the transparent things have in common? What do all opaque objects have in common?

Follow-up

• Make shadows from hands or objects – experiment with the shapes which can be made.
• Draw silhouettes of objects – shine a light onto them and trace round the shadow they make on a piece of paper.
• Make shadow puppets.

Reflection

Age range

Eight to nine.

Group size

Two to four.

What you need

A collection of shiny objects, a torch, bendy safety mirrors, white and black card.

Science content

Light can reflect off materials. Different surfaces reflect light to varying degrees. White surfaces reflect light well but dark surfaces absorb light. Some materials cause the light to become scattered or diffused when it hits them, whereas highly polished surfaces reflect most of the light in one specific direction.

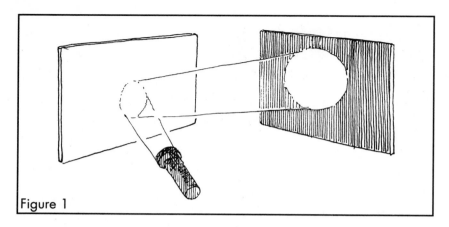

Figure 1

What to do

Ask the children to look at the objects. In which can they see their reflection? What do these objects have in common? What other objects in the room give a reflection?

Tell the children to shine the torch into a mirror at such an angle that it reflects on to one of the objects (Figure 1). How well is the light reflected on to that object? Test all the objects and the black and white card. What happens in each case? What is the difference in the brightness of the reflections? (Some materials absorb light and some diffuse it.) Sort the objects according to how well they reflect. Record the results with pictures or words.

Follow-up

• Conduct investigations with mirrors. Where do you need to hold the mirror to see behind you/round a corner/the ceiling?
• Draw a picture on paper and position the mirror so that you can see two of them, half of it and so on. Draw half a house and position the mirror to make a whole house.
• Challenge the children to make mirror cards with tasks for other children to try.
• Make a periscope.

How light travels

Age range
Eight to ten.

Group size
Two to four.

What you need
A torch, a shoe box, white paper, a craft knife, a darkened room, a safety mirror, a ruler, a pencil, a bottle covered in aluminium foil.

Science content
Light travels from its source in straight lines and can be reflected from some surfaces. The angle of incidence equals the angle of reflection.

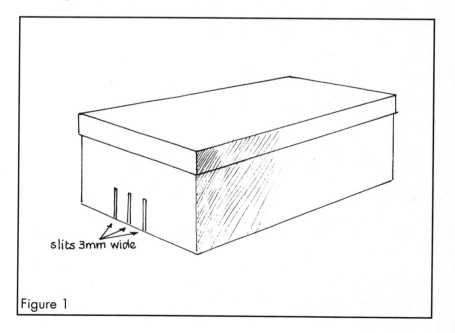

slits 3mm wide

Figure 1

What to do

Cut several thin slits in one end of a shoe box (approximately 3mm wide and 30mm long). See Figure 1. (*Safety:* You may need to do this for the children.) Place the torch inside the box and let its beam shine through the slits on to a piece of white paper. You may need a darkened room.

Look at the beams of light as they shine on the paper. What do you notice about them? Trace the edge of one of the lines. Lift up the paper. What do you notice? Is the line straight?

What happens to the beams of light if you place an object in between the box and piece of paper? What happens if you place a mirror in front of the beam? Try holding the mirror at different angles. What do you notice? Try a curved reflective surface such as the bottle covered with aluminium foil. What do you notice? Can you say why this happens?

Follow-up

Make a periscope or kaleidoscope.

How do we see?

Age range
Ten to eleven.

Group size
Whole class or small groups.

What you need
Photocopiable page 128, a pencil, a labelled diagram of the human eye, safety mirrors.

Science content
We see things when light reflected from them enters our eyes. The light enters the pupil, an opening in the coloured part of the eye, or iris. A lens behind the iris focuses the light on to the retina at the back of the eye. Special optical nerves then carry messages to the brain which interprets the image. See Figure 1.

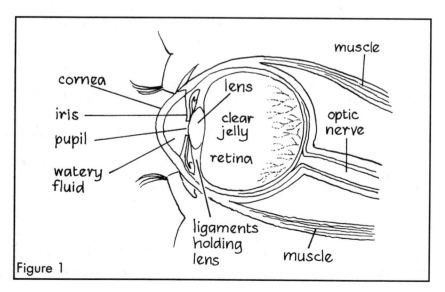

Figure 1

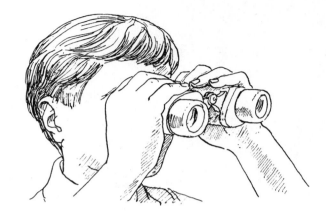

What to do
Explain to the children how our eyes are used for seeing things and how the eye works. Look at a diagram of the parts of the eye. Ask the children to use a safety mirror to look closely at their own eyes. What things do they notice?

Ask the children to look at photocopiable page 128 and then draw arrows to show how they think the person in each case sees the object. Discuss the results with a group of children or with the whole class. Do they agree? Some children may draw arrows from the eye to the object. This is a common misconception. No rays leave our eyes, we see things because light from the objects enters our eyes. You can help them to overcome this misconception by explaining that if rays came from our eyes, we would be able to see in the dark. The children could be encouraged to devise a test to prove this.

Follow-up
• Conduct an experiment to find out about blind spots.
• Carry out an eye test.
• Find out about colour-blindness.
• What do blind people use to 'see' the world?

Day and night

Age range
Eight to ten.

Group size
Small group or whole class.

What you need
A globe, a torch or projector, a small cut-out paper person, Blu-Tack.

Science content
The Earth takes 24 hours to rotate once on its axis. The sun shines on only one half of the world at any one time, creating day and night.

What to do
Attach the cut-out person to a place on the globe using Blu-Tack. Use a darkened room and shine the light on the globe. Which side of the world has 'daylight'? Why? Which side is in night? Why?

Spin the globe slowly anticlockwise and watch what happens to the light shining on the globe. Watch the figure on the globe to see how daylight changes into night for that person.

Follow-up
Make a study of world time zones. Discuss the implications of this for world travel.

The Moon

Age range
Ten to eleven.

Group size
Small group.

What you need
Pictures of the Sun, Earth and Moon; paper, pencil, card, scissors, compass, ruler, overhead projector, orange, stick or piece of dowelling.

Science content
The Moon is approximately 385,000 miles away from Earth and is small in comparison. It has a diameter of 3,476km compared with Earth's 12,756km diameter. Both are tiny in comparison with the Sun which has a diameter of 1,392,530km. The Moon takes approximately 28 days to orbit the Earth. We see the Moon, not because it emits light itself, but because light from the Sun hits it and is reflected back to us.

What to do
Look at the pictures of the Sun, Earth and Moon. Discuss the huge difference in their sizes. Make card models of the three using the following scale as an approximation of size:

(Scale: 1mm = 4880km)

Planet	Diameter
Sun	286mm
Earth	2.6mm
Moon	1mm

Use the models to explain how the Earth orbits the Sun and how the Moon orbits the Earth. Discuss the Moon in particular. What can the children tell you about the Moon? Have they seen the phases of the Moon? What names are used to describe them? (See the diagram below.) What causes these phases to occur?

Demonstrate how the Moon phases occur by asking a child to stand in the light of an overhead projector with her left shoulder facing towards the light. Push an orange on to a stick and ask the child to hold the stick in her right hand just above her head so that the light shines on the orange. Ask the child to turn slowly, anticlockwise, to see how the amount of light falling on the orange changes.

Ask the children to keep a daily diary of the Moon phases as a homework activity. How does the shape change? How long is it between full moons? Does the position of the Moon in the sky change?

Follow-up
Find out about the Apollo landings and the names of the plains and craters which have been named by scientists.

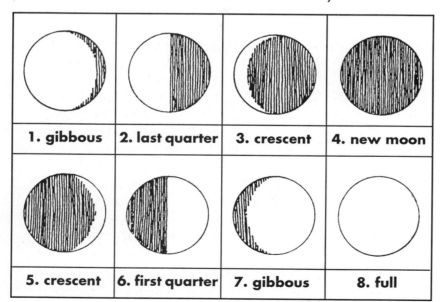

| 1. gibbous | 2. last quarter | 3. crescent | 4. new moon |
| 5. crescent | 6. first quarter | 7. gibbous | 8. full |

Space rocket

Age range
Nine to eleven.

Group size
Two to four.

What you need
Grey board or thick cardboard (21cm x 40cm x 2–3mm), a craft knife, 3 wide rubber bands (10mm wide), 2 ice-lolly sticks, a ruler, a pencil, a nail (2.5cm long), a small piece of chipboard, a coping saw, adhesive tape, Corriflute (optional), adhesive suitable for card or Corriflute, a balloon, pictures of rockets and launching pads, a drill.

Science content
Rockets need a huge amount of fuel to push themselves into space. The gas pushing downwards from the base of the rocket causes the rocket to move upwards in the opposite direction. This is what Isaac Newton describes as his Third Law – the action force and the reaction force are equal and opposite. The gain of momentum of the rocket is equal and opposite to the momentum of the hot gases that are escaping.

What to do
Ask the children to tell you how they think a rocket works. How is it able to travel so far up into space? Look at pictures of rockets, discuss what they are made of, what shapes they are and why. Look at pictures of launching pads – why are they so big and strong?

Explain that a rocket works in a similar way to when you blow up a balloon and let it go. Allow the children to do this. Ask them what is pushing the balloon forwards. Talk about how the escaping fuel in a rocket acts in the same way as air escaping from the balloon.

Now allow the children time to make a rocket and launch pad of their own by following the directions below:

Follow-up
Let the children design and make their own rockets using alternative means of propulsion – such as balloons or springs.

1. Rule lines on board 7cm apart. Using a craft knife, score along the lines to bend the card into a triangular shape. Use adhesive tape to join the edges together.

2. Make three holes about 4cm from the end of the tube. Push a rubber band through each hole and secure in place using half an ice-lolly stick.

3. Cut a piece of plywood to fit the tube. Drill a hole in the middle. Gather the three bands together and push through the hole. Secure with a nail.

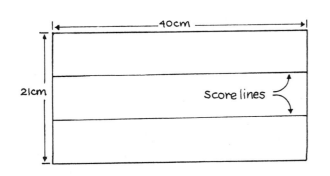

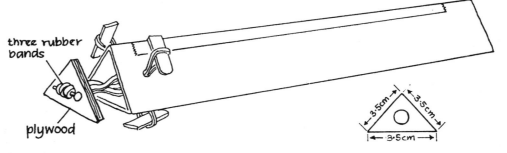

three rubber bands

plywood

3.5cm 3.5cm 3.5cm

4. Join two pieces of thick card or Corriflute together to make a rocket.
To work: push the rocket into the launch pad so it rests on the plywood deep inside. Let go!

31cm

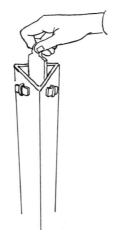

Safety: Supervise the launching of the rocket as it can travel a great distance. Do not allow the children to point it at people or at light fittings and so on. Make sure they point it away from themselves.

Discuss why the launching pad needs to be so deep. Why is a triangular shape used? Would round cardboard tubes work as well? Why/why not? If a lighter rocket was used, would it work as well? If the children have time, they could explore the answers to these questions themselves, using a variety of materials.

DISPLAY IDEAS

• Paint a large mural of the solar system and add the children's research about the planets.
• Make a collection of objects which produce light and display them alongside children's writing about light investigations.
• Cut out silhouettes of objects or the children's profiles and display them alongside their writing about shadow investigations.
• Paint a large mural of the same scene at night and in the day time. Add information about how day and night occur.
• Display the children's model rockets as mobiles.

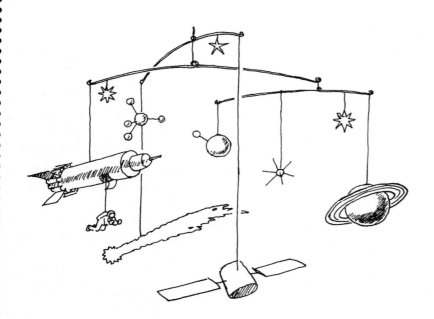

• Make a papier-mâché moonscape. Add moon buggy models made by the children and writing about how they made them.
• Paint the planets on the windows.
• Make story books about space travel and display these on a table. Mount information about the history of space travel on card behind the table and hang the children's model rockets around the display.
• Make a space station in the corner of the classroom from card and aluminium foil and attach the children's research about planets.
• Make and display shadow puppets on a table with the children's writing about shadow formation mounted on the wall behind the table.
• Turn one half of the room into day and one half into night using paintings on the walls and windows. Include models of things seen in the day and in the night.

Links with other curriculum areas

Geography
- The use of satellite photographs and aerial photographs – what the Earth looks like from space.
- Moon maps – names of craters.
- Navigation – using the stars.
- Star maps – constellations.
- Making a map of an alien place.

RE
- Myths and legends about gods.
- Creation stories.
- What is Heaven?

Music
- Listening to/singing songs about space.
- Making sounds of a rocket lift-off.
- Imagined music from other planets

Maths
- Large numbers.
- Measuring distances.
- Diameter and circumference.
- Scale of planets and distances in space.
- Countdowns.

Space

Technology
- Designing, making and evaluating a space rocket or moon buggy.
- Making scale models of planets.
- Using construction kits to make landing bases and rockets.
- Designing a spaceship or home on another planet.
- Designing an alien.
- Designing a space suit.

Art
- Painting night skies.
- Planet mobiles.
- Clay model rockets.
- Painting scenes from other planets.
- Making collages of the solar system.
- Moonscapes.

History
- The history of space travel – dates and names, countries involved.
- Myths and legends about gods.
- Developments in astronomy.

English
- Reading stories/ poems about space.
- Writing a story about travel to another planet.
- Descriptions of planets.
- Discussion – is space travel worth spending money on?
- Write a newspaper report about a UFO sighting.
- Role-play – aliens, astronauts.

115

Reproducible material

Body parts, see page 10

- Cut out the pieces of the jigsaw and join them together to make the shape of a person.

Me and my friend, see page 11

My name: _____

A drawing of my face

My friend's name: _____

A drawing of my friend's face

Colour of eyes: _____

Colour of skin: _____

Colour of hair: _____

Special features of face: _____

_____

_____

My height: _____

Colour of eyes: _____

Colour of skin: _____

Colour of hair: _____

Special features of face: _____

_____

_____

My friend's height: _____

Our bones, see page 16

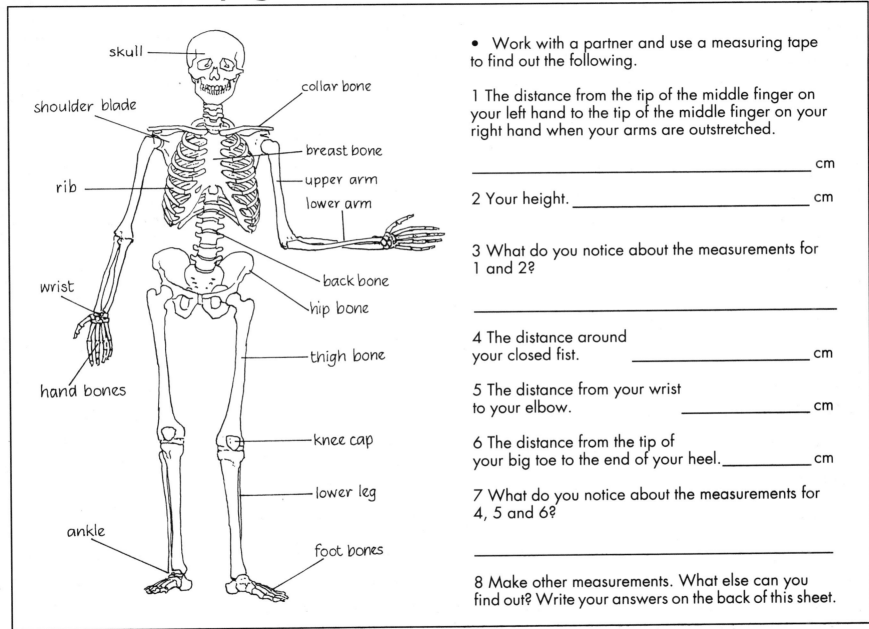

skull

collar bone

shoulder blade

breast bone

rib

upper arm

lower arm

wrist

back bone

hip bone

hand bones

thigh bone

knee cap

lower leg

ankle

foot bones

- Work with a partner and use a measuring tape to find out the following.

1 The distance from the tip of the middle finger on your left hand to the tip of the middle finger on your right hand when your arms are outstretched.

_____ cm

2 Your height. _____ cm

3 What do you notice about the measurements for 1 and 2?

_____

4 The distance around
your closed fist. _____ cm

5 The distance from your wrist
to your elbow. _____ cm

6 The distance from the tip of
your big toe to the end of your heel._____ cm

7 What do you notice about the measurements for 4, 5 and 6?

_____

8 Make other measurements. What else can you find out? Write your answers on the back of this sheet.

Name: _____

Conduct this survey about you and your family to find out if you lead a healthy lifestyle. Compare your answers with those of other children in your class.

1 How many times a week do you exercise?

2 Do you think this is enough?

3 What kinds of exercise do you do?

4 Which members of your family also exercise?

5 Do you ever exercise as a whole family?

6 If yes, what do you do?

7 Does anyone in your family smoke?

8 If yes, how does this affect you?

9 Do you think you will smoke when you get older?

Why/why not?

10 What do you eat for breakfast?

11 What do you usually eat for lunch?

12 Do you have an evening meal with your family?

What is your favourite meal?

13 Do you have fruit and vegetables every day?

14 What drinks do you usually have?

15 Do you always wash your hands before eating?

Why/why not?

16 Why is it important to wash your hands after patting an animal?

17 Why is it important to keep kitchens and bathrooms clean?

18 Is it safe to take someone else's medicine if you have the same illness?

19 Are drugs safe to use?

20 Is it safe to sniff glue?

21 Are you allergic to anything?

Sorting leaves, see page 26

- Examine your leaf carefully. Follow the branches on the tree diagram that describe your leaf and draw your leaf in the box you have reached.

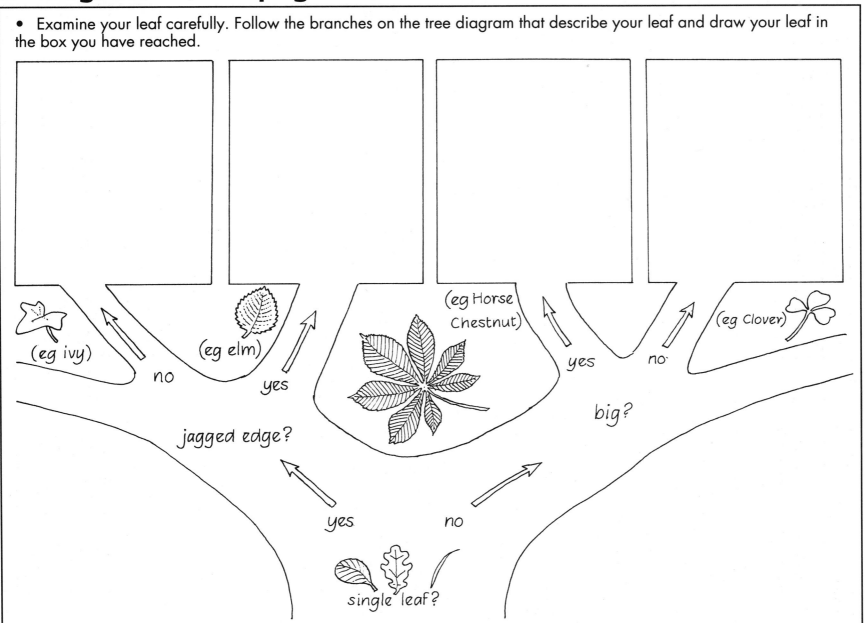

Where would you find it?, see page 27

- Cut out all the pictures of plants and animals below.
- Now match them with the habitats in which they live. Some may live in more than one habitat so find the one to which you think they would best be suited. When you have finished matching the pictures, stick the groups on to a large sheet of paper.
- Draw other living things of your own. Cut them out and add them to your groups.

duckweed

fieldmouse

oak tree

woodlouse

fungi

worm

hedgehog

habitat 1

in a pond

habitat 2

in a field

daisy

fly

habitat 3

under a log

habitat 4

on a tree

habitat 5

in a garden

rose bush

frog

squirrel

Flowering plant life cycle, see page 33

Where I found it:

Date:

Colour of petals:

Height of my flower:

What the stem is like:

How many?

A drawing of my flower:

A rubbing of a leaf:

A rubbing of a petal:

Pond study, see page 41

Name of animal	**Where did you find it?**
Sketch of animal	above the water ☐ near the middle ☐
	on the water ☐ on the rocks ☐
	in the water ☐ on plants ☐
	on the bottom ☐ among the reeds ☐
	Colour
	Size
	How does it move?
	Does the shape of the animal help it to move easily in the water?
How does it breathe?	
Does it come to the surface of the water?	
Can you suggest how it breathes?	Does it have special swimming fins or legs?
Eating Does it have any special eating aids on its body?	Any special features to be noted.
What do you think the animal eats?	

FISH OBSERVATION SHEET

Describe the fins

How many fins does the fish have?

Does your fish prefer to be in a group or on its own?

How wide is it?

Can you see any marks on the body?

Can you see your fish breathing?

What colour are the eyes?

What does the fish eat?

How long is it?

How does it breathe?

What colour is your fish?

Watch the tail fin move. Describe the movement.

What shape is the tail fin?

Does your fish rest?

Where does your fish prefer to be?

Watch closely how the fish moves. Can it go backwards? What helps it to move?

Levers, see page 81

• Which of the pictures below show examples of levers?

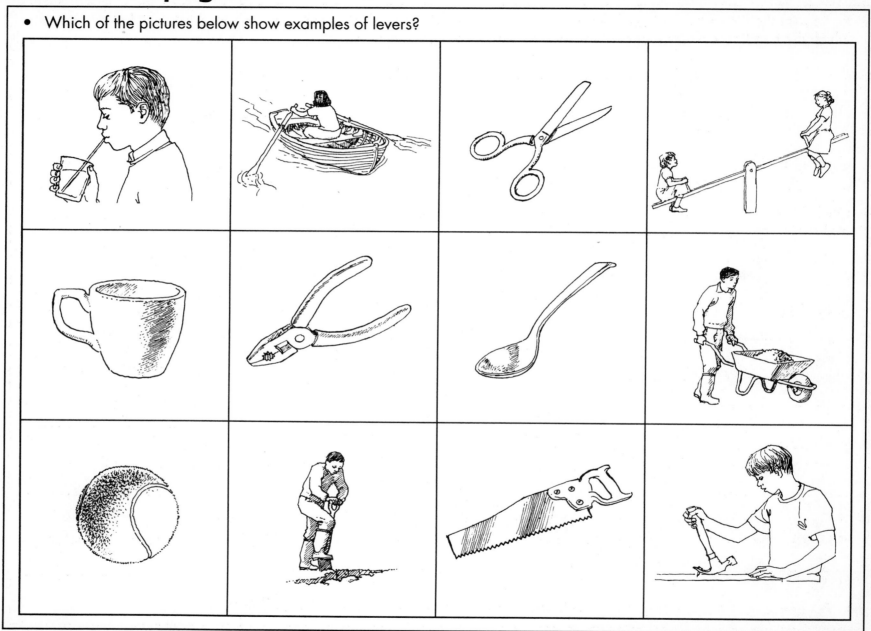

Sources of building materials, see page 99

• Look at the picture of a house below and then at the word box. Which word from the box describes the material of which the building part is made? Write your answer in the space provided.

sand	clay	bauxite	iron ore
trees	sandstone	oil	limestone and clay

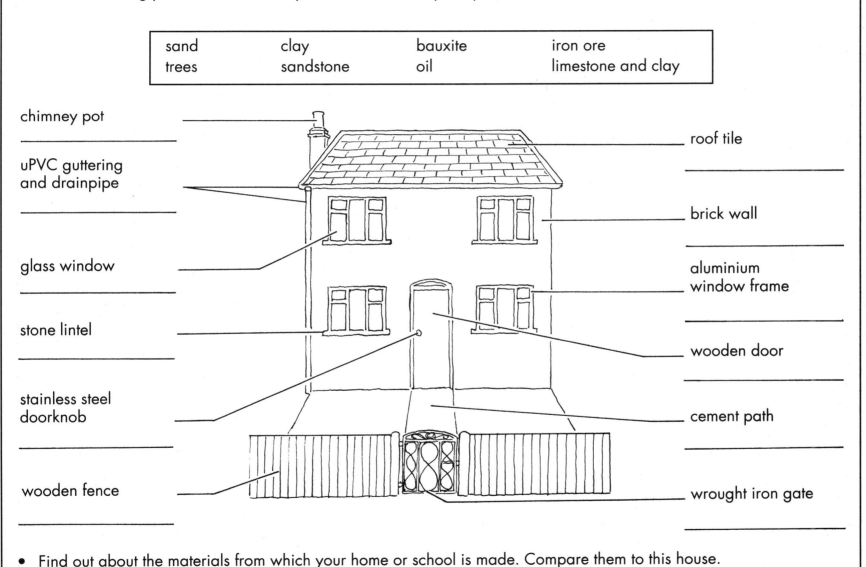

chimney pot
_____

uPVC guttering
and drainpipe
_____

glass window
_____

stone lintel
_____

stainless steel
doorknob
_____

wooden fence
_____

roof tile
_____

brick wall
_____

aluminium
window frame
_____

wooden door
_____

cement path
_____

wrought iron gate
_____

• Find out about the materials from which your home or school is made. Compare them to this house.

How do we see?, see page 110

Name: _____

- In each of the drawings below draw arrows to show how you think the person sees the object.
- Compare your answers with others in your class. Do they agree?